THE BRIGHT AND
BOLD DESIGN

THE BRIGHT AND BOLD DESIGN

by Peter Whelan

Warner Chappell Plays

LONDON

A Time Warner Company

First published in 1991
by Warner Chappell Plays Ltd
129 Park Street, London W1Y 3FA

Copyright © 1991 by Peter Whelan

ISBN 0 85676 144 3

Printed by Commercial Colour Press, London E7.

To Jack Price

The father-in-law I never met.

THE BRIGHT AND BOLD DESIGN was premièred by the Royal Shakespeare Company at the Barbican Pit, London on 26 November, 1991, with the following cast:

ULIK DEVLIN	Bill McGuirk
VIOLET CHAPPEL	Clare Lawrence
JESSIE FROST	Katy Behean
ADA LOVATT	Georgiana Dacombe
JOYCE MURRAY	Catherine White
HECTOR BRABANT	Paul Webster
JIM RHYS	Clive Russell
MABEL COOPER	Polly Kemp
GRACE RHYS	Alex Kingston
RAYMOND PARKER	Callum Dixon

Directed by	Bill Alexander
Designed by	Kit Surrey
Produced by	Nicky Pallot

FOREWORD

As a child in Stoke-on-Trent, it always seemed to me magical that you could earn a living by freehand painting pottery. Money for brush strokes . . .

The Paintresses were a legend then and still draw the crowds today at Wedgwood's Barlaston factory, where you can watch them at work in the entrance lobby. So when I read the brief details of the life of Clarice Cliff, the working class paintress who became a star designer in the 1930's, I was all attention. What is fascinating is the way her talents were brought to light and encouraged in a Svengali-like way by the man she worked for, Colly Shorter . . . who she eventually married. At first I thought about writing a play about them.

But it was another path that began to draw my thoughts. This process of shaping others to the shaper's image . . . what if there were resistance? What if the object of the shaper's obsession wished to control her own destiny?

Out of this, Jessie Frost cam into being. Like Clarice, a working class paintress. Like Clarice, promoted by the man she worked for. And, for that man, I had a model in my remarkable father-in-law, Jack Price, himself a talented pottery designer in the 1930's (His work is even now being re-discovered).

Significantly for me, he was also a force in local Labour politics . . . a thoughtful, mainstream socialist activist but one who, as in the play, was more than ready for the revolution to start in the middle of the night. I've always felt a sense of loss that he died before I could meet him. I also have the usual playwright's sense of guilt that I have made free with his character to make my play.

For the confrontation of Jessie and Jim goes far beyond the personal. They draw their energies from two different visions of the human struggle . . . Jim's is the struggle to improve and perfect society . . . Jessie's is the survival struggle of life itself.

The wilful reshaping of other people's destinies has played all too clear a role in the whirlwind violence of our century. The claims on the individual to commit to common causes and shared ideals have been all too powerful. And even from those with the best intentions the pressure has had a threatening edge.

It is these forces that are released in Jessie and Jim . . . with me, as I wrote the play, watching the tides of old certainties recede in the world . . . and writing in a mood of respect, not for the label or the theory or the gesture, but for the goodness and humanity of personal aspirations.

Morally, it's where we came in.

Peter Whelan
November, 1991

Technical Note

A technical contacts list has been compiled, including sources of advice on freehand pottery painting and the making up of sample ware. It also contains details of flat art designs and pottery samples available from the original Royal Shakespeare Company production . . . plus the Ovaltine jingle music.

For further information please apply to the author through his agents.

ACT ONE

Scene One

North Staffordshire in the 1930's. The freehand decorating shop of Hector Brabant and Company, a small "Pot Bank" or pottery firm near Burslem. The lofty interior of flaking, colour-washed brick and tall, grimy windows has the upwardly soaring lines of a Victorian school room. Down at bench level there is chaotic life in the rough jumble of vases, tea pots, tea services and jugs. Most are painted with pastel shaded floral designs. One or two pieces of blank white ware await the freehold painter's skill. But we see this only faintly in the dimness of an early March morning.

Now the sparse electric lights are turned on by ULIK DEVLIN. *He is a wasted man with the rough, scarred look of an alcoholic. He crosses to the small designer's office, separated by a half-glazed partition, and turns on the light. This room is bare, with boxes piled up, as though packing had taken place recently.*

The first of the paintresses now arrives, the apprentice, VIOLET CHAPPEL. ULIK *stares at her. Neither speaks. He takes his time. Stops to look at the work on* JESSIE FROST'S *bench, then goes.* VIOLET *has taken off her things and put on an overall, and she now gets down to work in a troubled, urgent way. She removes an upturned saucer from a tile on her desk and adds turps and fat-oil to the moist colour, mixing it with a palette knife. Then she starts painting petals on a blank plate. When she hears a sound she puts the work aside with a secretive air.*

Enter JESSIE FROST *in coat and scarf. She is not pleased that* VIOLET *is here before her, liking to have the place to herself first thing.*

JESSIE	I saw your shadow from the yard.
VIOLET	All I did was come in . . .
JESSIE	I always look up when I come through the gates. I thought someone's been in before me. Some bird's caught the worm!
VIOLET	Am I not supposed to?

JESSIE	Anything that moves in here casts a little faint wobble up there. Like a magic lantern.
VIOLET	I didn't turn on the electric . . .

(*She is embattled.*)

JESSIE	So! I've got competition at getting in first, have I? I shall have to stir myself sooner . . . not dawdle and doze . . .
VIOLET	I found a quicker way to get here. By Hope Street. It's got more shelter from the rain.
JESSIE	I didn't notice it raining. (*She knows it wasn't.*)
VIOLET	When it does, I mean.
JESSIE	Well . . . it is threatening.

(VIOLET *makes a show of settling to her work as though it wasn't the reason that brought her in early.* JESSIE *glances through the window.*)

And who'd believe that orange in the clouds?

(*She picks up a pot of orange colour.*)

There's more fire in that than this one. Yet if you did clouds that colour people would say: "don't be daft! The sky's never like that!"

VIOLET	(*squinting at her work*) Heck!
JESSIE	How are your petals?
VIOLET	Oh . . .
JESSIE	Will they pass muster?
VIOLET	I was at it ever so late.
JESSIE	They'll come in time.

VIOLET	I've only got till today to get them right. I could hardly see last night.

JESSIE   D'you have gas?

VIOLET   (*ashamed*) Yes . . . no one has electric down our road.

                   (JESSIE *softens towards her a little.*)

JESSIE   Shall I do some with you? Before she gets here.

                   (*Alongside at the bench she takes up unpainted ware.*)

VIOLET   My hand won't stay still.

JESSIE   Keep calm. Your colour's a bit thickish. Thin it a bit more. Get more pink in your pencil.

                   (*She adds turps and fat-oil to the colour on the mixing tile.*)

VIOLET   It'll blob.

JESSIE   You won't let it. Keep on the move and it won't. Lean more on the upward stroke and get the little twist more sudden.

VIOLET   I can't think what it is I'm doing different.

JESSIE   You're nearly there. Do another. More paint. Bend the bristles. Lean your pencil.

VIOLET   You use such funny words here. Why'd you call a brush a pencil?

JESSIE   Because we're the paintresses! We're "it", don't ye know? No ordinary words for us! We walk on God's earth without touching it. Even if we do all stink of turps. And if we want to call a brush a pencil we will call a brush a pencil.

(*As she speaks* JESSIE *holds a plate and, turning it, paints the petals at a smooth, steady pace.*)

VIOLET   I can never go that fast!

JESSIE   As you turn the plate your hand's ready for the next . . .

VIOLET   Yes but . . .

JESSIE   See it in your mind and your fingers will follow.

VIOLET   That's one!

JESSIE   Keep it up . . . settle. Relax . . .

VIOLET   I'm doing it!

JESSIE   Don't lean with your body. See it in your mind . . .

VIOLET   Oh heck!

JESSIE   Gently . . . bit faster.

VIOLET   Oh mother!

JESSIE   Go on . . .

VIOLET   Oh! Oh!

JESSIE   One more . . .

VIOLET   I've done it!

(JESSIE *examines the plate.*)

JESSIE   Yes. I'd pay for that.

(*Enter* ADA LOVATT, *the charge hand.*)

ADA   Has Ulik brought the ware down? Oh, Jessie he hasn't! He'll be asleep somewhere.

VIOLET   No. He was here . . . He turned on the electric.

(ADA *gives her a quick sharp look.*)

JESSIE	She was first in today.
ADA	How can we work without nothing to work on? How can we earn? I shall report him.
JESSIE	Ada . . .
ADA	I'm not going to be soft about it. I have to make my money if you don't. Oh he does vex me! He should ask me each evening what we need. I'm supposed to be in charge. He just won't recognise it.

(*Enter* JOYCE MURRAY, *yawning.*)

JOYCE	Are we going on about Ulik? We haven't even started the day!
ADA	(*to* VIOLET) Violet! Did he say he was bringing it?
VIOLET	He didn't say nothing.
ADA	Nothing?
VIOLET	No. Nothing.
JOYCE	Good morning Jessie.
JESSIE	Good morning Joyce.
ADA	He knows I'm not given the backing from above. And if I'm not backed why should he care?
JESSIE	He'll come. He just won't be governed, Ada. You know he won't. .
ADA	Won't he? Well I shall say something . . . I shall.
JOYCE	Oh . . . Michaelmas daisies! Plink, Plink, plonk! How much did we say for plates?

ADA	Eighteens.
JOYCE	And jugs?
ADA	Sevens.
JOYCE	Sevens! And they call that fair!
ADA	It's what it is!
JOYCE	It's a mistake! You can't do seven to the dozen. Not for sixpence. I won't make my money this week. Nor will you.
JESSIE	Come on you two sunbeams! It is Saturday . . .
JOYCE	Then why does it feel like Monday?
JESSIE	Well it's a bit dark and dreary . . .
JOYCE	And down! I feel so down! I shouldn't feel down on Saturday! Monday you're bound to feel down. Everyone knows you do. Tuesday's good. You feel uplifted again, mainly by having got over Monday! Wednesday's the worst, when you realise you've got the rest of the week to work. Thursday you're nothing. You're numb. You're nowhere. But Friday - you see - Friday you're up! You're thinking of freedom! You're fluttering your feathers and ready to fly - then you wake up and you've still got half of Saturday to come. And that's why it feels like Monday.
JESSIE	Saturday's the baths.
JOYCE	Going with Mab?
JESSIE	Yes.
JOYCE	Must be nice, sharing.
JESSIE	The baths?
JOYCE	Your place. Your flat.

JESSIE	We can bicker a bit, but who cares?
	(*A silence as they all work.* VIOLET *is getting ready to show what she's done.*)
ADA	I had a boiled egg this morning.
VIOLET	Miss Lovatt . . .
JOYCE	Just a minute. Quiet please. Go on, Ada. You had a boiled egg this morning . . .
ADA	I have been told you can get everything you need from a boiled egg.
JOYCE	You what?
ADA	It's true.
JOYCE	It isn't.
ADA	It is.
JOYCE	Who says?
ADA	Doctors.
JOYCE	Doctors? Doctors? Well I can't get everything I need from a boiled egg!
VIOLET	Could you have a look at my petals?
JOYCE	Hello!
ADA	After I've spoken to Ulik.
JOYCE	Do we all get a look at her petals?
ADA	Joyce!
JOYCE	Well! She's not been what d'you call it has she? Not had her oo-jah. Her ceremony. Initiation. We all had to go through our ceremonies didn't we? Look at her! You won't be so uppity with your bum in a pan of raspberry jam.

(*Enter* ULIK DEVLIN. *He pushes a trolley loaded with unpainted ware.*)

JESSIE	Oh Ulik!
ULIK	Heyup!
JOYCE	You're for it!
ULIK	For what?
ADA	For being so late.
ULIK	Who says?
JESSIE	You are you know.
ULIK	(*indicating* ADA) Does her think I'm late? Does her?
JOYCE	Tell him.
ULIK	Who's late? Who's late? They's got were theer to last hafe an hour. So who's late?
JOYCE	Well, Ada has something to say to you.
ULIK	And I've somethin to say to her . . .
JOYCE	Ladies first.
ADA	No. Let him speak if he's going to speak. It'll make a change him speaking.
ULIK	Right. Mr Brabant's coming ter say they.
ADA	When?
ULIK	In a bit.
ADA	What for?
ULIK	To bring thi new gaffer. The new art director.
JOYCE	That's Monday, surely?

ULIK	I've seed him. I've seed him. An I know who he is.
JOYCE	Who?
ULIK	They't find out.
JOYCE	Mr Rhys?
ULIK	They wusner gerrit from may.
JOYCE	Wunner ah? How uncouth. You talk like a cart-horse.
ULIK	I didner know carthosses spoke.
JOYCE	You ask him Jessie. He'll tell you.
ULIK	Not even her. (*To* JESSIE.) Didst see the sky this morning then?
JESSIE	I did.
ULIK	God's an artist. Eh?
	(*He goes, taking the painted ware that is ready to go.* ADA *begins to tidy up.*)
JOYCE	I know who it is.
ADA	Who?
JOYCE	I've told you. Mr Rhys from Cauldons. It's been settled for a fortnight. They know in the office, don't they Jessie?
ADA	Well no one's told us!
JESSIE	Maybe he'll wake things up a bit.
JOYCE	He can't do worse than Cyril.
ADA	Mr Hancock is dead!
JOYCE	Then he can't do worse.

ADA	You have no feelings for anyone.
JESSIE	Ada, that's not true.

(*A silence. They work on with feelings of tension.* JOYCE *is upset but won't show it.*)

VIOLET	What about these?
ADA	What?
VIOLET	My petals . . .

(*Enter* HECTOR BRABANT, *showing in* JIM RHYS.)

HECTOR	This is it. Good morning ladies.
ALL	Morning sir!
HECTOR	Good morning! If I could have a moment of your time . . .
JOYCE	Would you like a seat sir? (*After an uncomprehending pause.*) To sit down on.
HECTOR	I don't think so. Not at the moment, since I wish to say a word before . . . about our departed late Head of Design. Well now . . . (*Loudly.*) . . . De mortuis nisi bonum est! The Lord giveth and we are as dust. Let us think for a moment of Cyril Hancock gone on before, taken in his prime. Let none speak ill. This was our brother who has prematurely journeyed to another shore. And let none spread hearsay or rumour. However . . .

(*He turns from the prayerful attitude and smiles at* JIM, *wondering if he's done the right thing in appointing him.*)

. . . all shall be replaced. The old with the new, the known with the unknown . . . the familiar with the strange . . . the unfamiliar. And so we welcome Mr Rhys. Rhys. That is R-h-y-s, Rhys . . .

not R-e-e-s, Rees, like the other Mr Rees in our accounts office.

(*He leaves an awkward pause.*)

JIM   Good morning.

ALL   Morning sir.

HECTOR   Mr Rhys is come amongst us from Cauldons to be our new art director. You will find he has particular views. Very particular. His own views. We are not all made the same way, are we?

JOYCE   No sir.

HECTOR   Thank goodness. It is to the glory of the human race that we are not . . .

             (MABEL COOPER *enters with a note. She hovers till he notices her.*)

             But this I will say: Mr Rhys has the right to expect and to be given at all times . . . (*To* MAB.) Yes?

MAB   Mr Savage asks if you would look at this.

             (*He reads it and frowns. He is inwardly glad of an excuse to get away.*)

HECTOR   It seems as though I have a matter that must be considered right away. (*To* JIM.) So I'll leave you a moment in your new domain. If Miss Cooper would also stay and see you back to my office when you're ready. (*To the others.*) Well let us remember. That is all we can do. Bear in mind . . . (*He stops groping for more phrases and exits. The twinkle in* JIM's *eye is caught by* JOYCE.)

JOYCE   Hello.

JIM   Hello. Who are you?

JOYCE   Joyce Murray.

ADA   (*cutting in quickly*) I'm Ada Lovatt. I was put in
                charge by Mr Hancock.

JOYCE   She's the missus.

JIM   Ah! The missus!

ADA   Well, it's never really been acknowledged. I'll
                introduce everyone shall I? Joyce Murray.

JIM   What d'you do, Joyce?

JOYCE   You mean here? I'm a paintress.

ADA   She's a paintress.

JIM   For how long?

JOYCE   Four years.

ADA   This is Jessie Frost.

JIM   Ah! You're Jessie Frost. Burslem Art School?

JESSIE   Yes . . .

JIM   I've heard about you. And who's this?

ADA   Violet Chappel . . . apprentice.

                (JIM *bends over her work*.)

JIM   And what's she on?

VIOLET   Petals.

ADA   She's been learning the petals.

JIM   Good strokes.

VIOLET   I tried it a bit different today and suddenly it came
                to me.

                (JIM *catches the 'hard-faced' tone*. JESSIE *notes
                how the help she gave is not acknowledged*.)

ADA	(*miffed*) They do seem improved.
JIM	Does this line sell?
JOYCE	Mab can tell you. She's in sales.
MAB	I wouldn't say it does more than tick over. Less and less, really. This is a repeat for a group of shops in Holland. They like it.
JIM	Odd colour.
	(JOYCE, JESSIE *and* MAB *are amused.*)
ADA	It's as specified . . . It's how Mr Hancock said.
JOYCE	(*putting on her innocent air*) Haven't you ever seen Michaelmas daisies the colour of pork sausages?
	(JIM *grins. They all relax. He looks through to the designer's office.*)
JIM	Is this my office?
ADA	Yes sir.
JIM	I've interrupted you long enough. I'm not here to make speeches or get in your hair. The future's rushing down on us and there are things to do. Hand painted earthenware is what today is about. Colour that people can afford. Clear colour. Designs that take hold of what's happening in the world. Copeland and Maddocks got their streamlined dinner were on the Cunard liners to New York! I want ours in the air . . . on the flying boats, over the oceans! Look at Wilkinsons . . . Clarice Cliff . . . square tea pots and triangular saucers . . . everybody laughs but everyone takes notice. And people can feel the electricity of change in a tea cup or a salt pot. They can! So no speeches. I have made a speech. I'm sorry. No I'm not. I'll see you on Monday.

(*He exits.*)

JOYCE   Well what was all that then? I've lost threepence listening to that! I thought he was going to burst out crying at one point. Oh but I could see more of him. Doesn't he stand well! I like a man who can get on his back legs and stand! And what has he heard about you Jessie?

JESSIE   I know who he must be now. He's that friend my old art teacher used to mention.

ADA   He looked right past me. Right past.

VIOLET   I don't understand. Did he like my petals or not?

(*The lights fade.*)

Scene Two

The same at the end of the morning's work. It's Saturday going home time. JESSIE *and* MAB *are alone in the freehand shop dressed ready to go, but deep in a conversation that has shaken* JESSIE *badly.*

JESSIE   What will you do if they sack you?

MAB   I'll go mental!

JESSIE   What will *I* do?

MAB   Oh Jessie! I couldn't say a word when I was in here and there was Brabant and Mr Rhys.

JESSIE   But it wasn't Brabant was it? It *was* Mr Savage who told you?

(MAB *nods. Enter* VIOLET, *coated and scarved, for a forgotten glove. She finds it and goes in her customary embattled not speaking vein.*)

MAB   (*after* VIOLET *has gone*) Tara! Does she ever give utterance?

JESSIE   What did he say to you?

MAB   That I'd cheeked him. That I was 'pushy'. They
          all say 'pushy' cos I'm from Manchester. If you're
          not from the Potteries you're pushy. Ooooh!

JESSIE   But I still don't understand. Tell me. You went
          and spoke to Mr Savage?

MAB   Yes, I mean he's Sales Director, isn't he? I've
          been brooding over it for weeks. I told you!
          Suddenly I thought: now's the time. I thought I
          shall lay before him what it is I want to do and
          what it is I really came here for. So I said: Mr
          Savage, I have passed my commercial course by
          correspondence, and passed it well. I have
          French . . . he knows I have French cos I help
          with translating . . . I am taking commercial
          Spanish. I have been round twice with Mr
          Eardsley in the Leeds area and now I want to be
          a traveller. For Brabants. A commercial traveller.
          And I thought: it's Saturday so he's got Sunday to
          think over it . . . or if it all goes badly I've got
          Sunday to get over it.

JESSIE   And it went badly?

MAB   Well the nub of it was: Pigs may fly! "You're a
          lady, Miss Cooper". I thought: here we go! "And
          if you were a traveller you would have to
          entertain our customers who are all gentlemen."
          Not strictly true and he knows it . . . White's near
          Bradford is owned by a women and no one does
          anything without she says so. But let it pass. "Of
          course" he says "I wouldn't take it amiss because
          I know you." I thought: does he? "But most
          people would think it improper for you to be in
          bars, alone in strange towns, with gentlemen."

JESSIE   And what did you say?

MAB   I said: what d'you think I'm going to do to them?
          Now he was cunning. He said: "It's not what I
          think, or what the gentlemen might think . . . it's

what their wives may think!" Oh yes! Hey . . . and he also said: was I sure I could cope with some of these gentlemen?

JESSIE   Meaning some of them wouldn't be gentlemen.

MAB   Well I could see I'd practically lost by now, so I said, "Well, where men are concerned I can take the rough with the smooth. You have to don't you?" Then I went off like a rocket. He started turning all colours and my voice got to the pitch where it nearly rattled the cup off his saucer. So he went and told Brabant.

          (JOYCE *pops her head in as she's going.*)

JOYCE   Glad someone's laughing. Tata, duck!

JESSIE   And you duck!

JOYCE   Going swimming?

JESSIE   We were . . .

          (*She glances enquiringly at* MAB.)

MAB   We still are. (*To* JOYCE.) You come.

JOYCE   In bathing costumes?

MAB   You don't get in without.

JOYCE   Is it mixed?

JESSIE   Oh yes.

JOYCE   I don't go much for mixed bathing. I haven't got the knees. Tata!

          (*She exits.*)

JESSIE   She looks after her elder brother. Takes him out on Saturdays.

MAB   What's wrong with him?

JESSIE Lost part of his stomach in the war.

(*A silence.*)

MAB So. If I'm to be sacked, I'll have to count the pennies. Better not go to the Regent for tea. I'll get some angel cake.

JESSIE And Brabant hasn't spoken?

MAB No. Doesn't countenance me. He can never talk to anyone straight anyway. He'll get Savage to do it.

JESSIE Oh, I've been asleep to all this! I've never thought of them sacking someone.

MAB Jessie, they're sacking all the time!

JESSIE But if you should go . . . If you should go back to Manchester . . . there's no one else I could share with. And I can't manage the rent on my own-io. I can't go back home. Six of us in that steamy little hole. And if my mother went the same way as Joyce's, which she could . . . it'd be me! I know it'd be me! I'd cave in and crawl back. Which would be goodbye to everything . . .

MAB I'm not going back to Manchester. Either I'll eat humble pie or maybe I'll take Savage's advice. "If you want to be a female traveller do it in feminine products." He said the world's crying out for corset fitters . . . I said I shouldn't wonder.

JESSIE So you'll still be there?

(MAB *nods.* JESSIE *touches her arm.*)

I've never been happier in my life than in the last few months.

(*Enter* JIM RHYS *with two large boxes. He puts them down and smiles. He doesn't speak,*

appearing to concentrate on controlling his
breathing - very quietly and easily.)

MAB   Hello Mr Rhys.

JIM   A moment.

JESSIE   Are you alright?

JIM   Don't worry . . .

MAB   Shall I take these?

           (*She lifts the boxes. He nods.*)

JIM   Undo 'em.

           (*They wrestle with the string.*)

JESSIE   I've realised that you must know Mr McCloud . . .
           my art teacher.

JIM   (*recovering*) He taught me.

JESSIE   That's how you knew I was at Burslem Art
           School.

JIM   I know more than that!

JESSIE   What? What did he say?

JIM   Well, he said you had a devil in you . . .

JESSIE   Oh did he?

JIM   And I should be warned not to get on the wrong
           side of you. Though it's hard to know which side
           that is, he said.

MAB   Ahah! We should all like the answer to that.

JESSIE   He was one of these men who was always trying
           to get under your guard.

JIM   He also said I should value your imagination and skill.

                       (JESSIE *is embarrassed.*)

MAB   You should! She's wasted here.

JIM   Let's take those in. Just a few things for my new abode.

                       (*He carries the opened boxes into his new inner office.* JESSIE *and* MAB *follow, uncertainly.*)

MAB   Oh this dreadful dust. They should have done it out for you.

JESSIE   It's the same in the shop. Dust and rust. It gets in the colours.

JIM   I'm used to it. Aren't we all? That's the Potteries! Out of the filth we bring forth beauty. Now! The first thing to do is to take a good look at the opposition.

                       (*He unwraps and ranges out various jugs, vases, bowls and plates.* JESSIE *picks one out.*)

JESSIE   That's Wilkinsons . . .

MAB   They certainly go for the vivid.

JIM   Clarice Cliff's Bizarre Ware. Woman designer, hm? They're everywhere . . . Clarice, Susie Cooper, Charlotte Rhead, Millicent Taplin at Wedgwoods . . .

                       (MAB *holds a piece of Clarice Cliff ware.*)

MAB   D'you like it?

JESSIE   I do, yes.

MAB   A bit loud.

JIM   As the trumpet must be that blows down the walls
               of Jericho.

JESSIE   We'd never dash on the strokes like that . . .
               showing the bristle marks.

JIM   That's her cleverness. That says 'hand painted'.

               (*He and* JESSIE *smile at one another with
               understanding.* MAB *feels excluded.*)

MAB   My bag and things are still in the office. I'll get
               them before they lock up.

               (*She goes.* JIM *gives* JESSIE *a long appraising
               look, half smiling. She stares back.*)

JIM   Robbie McCloud said you had a steady hand and
               a steady eye.

JESSIE   Did he also say I couldn't be outstared?

JIM   He said you enjoyed making a mystery about
               yourself.

JESSIE   I'm not commenting on that.

JIM   That proves it then.

               (JIM *is the first to break off the staring contest. He
               unwraps another piece.*)

JESSIE   Who's that by?

JIM   Someone I used to know.

JESSIE   Is it yours?

JIM   It's not the way I want to go now.

JESSIE   I like it.

JIM	That was my William Morris period. The Utopian dream! Well . . . now we have to be wide awake. D'you ever do any designs?
JESSIE	I've made 'suggestions'.
JIM	Any taken up?
JESSIE	Er . . . taken up and twisted.
JIM	Robbie still has your work on display at Burslem. I'll give you every chance.
JESSIE	I'm only a paintress.
JIM	So was Clarice Cliff. There was a design of yours on Robbie's wall - a half drop repeat of saxophones. I liked it. Very dynamic and modern. Could you adapt it to a tea set?
JESSIE	What shape?
JIM	It would have to be out of the warehouse.
JESSIE	You'd need very upright cups. But we've got those. The Carpathia shape.
JIM	Try it. And keep the freedom in your strokes. (*Indicates Michaelmas daisies.*) Not like this stuff. We've got to catch the moment. We've got to inspire! We must lift people! There's no call to arms in Michaelmas daisies!
JESSIE	Oh? Does it have to be a call to arms? Where's the war?
JIM	Look around you, Jessie. Where isn't there a war?
	(MAB *re-enters, with her things.*)
MAB	Are you staying, Mr Rhys? I'll tell Tom not to shut you in.

JESSIE   We're going swimming.

MAB   We always make a splash on Saturdays.

JIM   Good for you. You can be at peace, swimming. I
                  used to think you were never more at one with
                  yourself than when you were under water . . .
                  when I used to do it.

JESSIE   Don't you now?

                  (*He doesn't answer.*)

JIM   Monday then! Monday we start.

JESSIE   Monday!

MAB   Monday . . . (*To herself.*) If I'm still here.

                  (*The lights fade.*)

Scene Three

*The garden of "The Pines", JIM RHYS'S Victorian red-bricked
detached house on the outskirts of the Potteries, beside a
plantation of pine trees. JIM'S wife GRACE is hacking away at the
soil with a hoe. She wears a film-star fashion of riding breeches
and thick white sweater and a Garbo broad brimmed hat. She
smokes and coughs as she works. Presently a dog begins barking
briskly from the garden. She calls to it.*

GRACE   Marx! Marx! Marx! Oh . . . shut up Marx! Will you
                  be silent! Cease! Cease! I said shut up!

                  (*A silence. Then more barking.*)

                  Marx! I don't want to hear from you any more!

                  (*Unseen by her,* HECTOR BRABANT *has entered
                  the garden and stands watching.*)

And don't dig the garden up . . . I've hoed that
bit! Gerroutofit! You mangy mongrel! You tyke!
You rotten rammel!

(*A pause. Silence. She is alarmed.*)

What have you got? What have you dug up?
Don't bring it over here! Take it away and bury
it. Take it away or you'll feel my boot. Take it
away!

HECTOR	Mrs Rhys?
GRACE	Yes . . .
HECTOR	I'm Hector Brabant.
GRACE	Are you really? Good heavens!

(*She is flustered. He shakes hands.*)

HECTOR	Having trouble with the dog?
GRACE	He's gone to post his letters. (*Realising.*) Oh him! He's dug up something awful over there. No, no! I don't want to see it.
HECTOR	It's an old glove.
GRACE	Glove? In the ground? Well I don't know what's buried under here. There could be corpses for all I know. I could have just buried my husband.
HECTOR	Will Jim be back?
GRACE	If he hasn't fallen down a hole. He's taken his car, so anything can happen.
HECTOR	I didn't want to burst in on you like this but I couldn't telephone . . .
GRACE	We don't have a telephone.
HECTOR	No. That's why I . . .

GRACE   We're getting one. A cream one. Next week.

HECTOR   If I can wait a little for him . . .

GRACE   (*a touch flirtatious*) You'll have to put up with me
                 like this.

HECTOR   Have you been riding?

                 (GRACE *is genuinely puzzled. What she wears
                 has nothing, in her mind, to do with horses.*)

GRACE   No.

                 (HECTOR *changes tack.*)

HECTOR   Ah yes! It's nearly spring!

GRACE   (*realising*) You mean my breeches. D'you think
                 women shouldn't wear them?

HECTOR   Oh I'm not out of the ark, Mrs Rhys.

GRACE   I didn't say you were.

HECTOR   I think they look splendid on the right figure.
                 And . . . er . . . well . . . yours look splendid.

GRACE   I did have to tailor them a little.

HECTOR   I've been trying to persuade my wife into
                 trousers.

GRACE   Won't she wear them?

HECTOR   She's a bit nervous of them.

GRACE   There's nothing to be afraid of in trousers!

                 (*A pause, the line of conversation having
                 exhausted itself.*)

HECTOR   We've been very pleased to take Jim aboard, Mrs
                 Rhys.

GRACE   He's pleased. Well, I think he's pleased. I haven't asked him. I wouldn't ask him. But the way he goes about shows he's pleased. He'd be whistling everywhere, if he whistled. He doesn't whistle. I do. He doesn't like me whistling. My name's Grace.

HECTOR   Grace. Of course.

GRACE   Of course?

HECTOR   He mentioned it to me. That you were Grace. And that your family were potters.

GRACE   I don't know what you mean by potters. My father was a kiln fireman at Johnsons and two of my female cousins got lead poisoning.

HECTOR   D'you know of John Harcourt?

GRACE   John Harcourt? He was at Spode.

HECTOR   Retired last year. I tried to get him to do a spell with us but he said, quite rightly, he'd had his innings. He told me if I wanted the most promising and most overlooked talent in the potteries to go for Jim Rhys. So . . . I lean on John Harcourt's judgement as you'd lean on an oak. And . . . (*He falters.*) I'm sure in the end it will prove correct. Even as we get to know one another . . .

GRACE   You and Jim?

HECTOR   Yes.

GRACE   But you've met!

HECTOR   Yes, of course we've met, Grace. We've met several times. But I'm talking of knowing someone properly. I've met you now, but I'm not going to pretend I know all about you.

GRACE   I hope nobody knows all about me!

HECTOR   Why? D'you have a guilty conscience?

GRACE   No. But I like my privacy.

HECTOR   Well there you are! I don't mean private things,
          oh no, no, no! I mean: you can think you know
          someone, and then you talk to someone else
          about them and it's like adding another colour to a
          pattern . . . it comes out quite different. And you
          think: maybe I don't know this man at all!

GRACE   Oh, I don't know Jim at all. There are times I'd be
          sitting there at night listening to the sounds . . .
          there are some awful sounds round here . . .
          owls and nightjars and animals coughing in the
          woods . . . and he'll come through the door and
          I'll think who on earth's this? And it's him!

HECTOR   What was it you were calling your dog, just now?

GRACE   I was being very rude to him, wasn't I?

HECTOR   I mean his name. Was it "Marx"?

          (GRACE *becomes guarded. She's embarrassed by
          the name in his presence.*)

GRACE   Yes.

HECTOR   That's his name . . . Marx?

GRACE   It's what we call him . . . well, what Jim called him.

HECTOR   How is it spelled?

GRACE   (*wary*) M . . . a . . . r . . . x . . .

HECTOR   After the famous brothers?

GRACE   I didn't know he had a brother!

          (*The sound of a car arriving and turning into the
          drive is heard.*)

          That's him . . . I'll warn him you're here . . .

HECTOR   Warn him?

GRACE   In case he gets out saying dreadful things about you!

(She laughs and exits. The dog barks as it races to meet the car. HECTOR *follows it suspiciously with his eye. Enter* JIM *followed by* GRACE.)

JIM   I'm sorry I wasn't here . . .

HECTOR   I'm sorry to interrupt a weekend, Jim, but I've had a last minute change to an appointment which means I won't be in on your first day on Monday. So I thought I'd erupt upon you briefly.

JIM   I see. Has Grace been entertaining you?

GRACE   I wouldn't say that!

JIM   No tea?

GRACE   I was waiting for you! I can't talk and make tea! I'll make it. Don't worry!

HECTOR   Before you do . . . I know this is a helter skelter arrangement . . . but we have an exhibition soon in Birmingham and I'd like Jim to come down on Wednesday, returning rather late.

GRACE   He can go where he likes. I'm not stopping him.

(She exits to the house. The dog barks.)

HECTOR   I was just trying to smooth the path . . . warning her you'd be late. Is that alright?

JIM   Yes, yes.

HECTOR   You must be very proud of her . . .

JIM   Er . . .

HECTOR	You won't mind me saying, but she looks as though she'd stepped right off the silver screen.
JIM	Don't tell her that!
HECTOR	Why not?
JIM	She lives enough of her life in a story.

(HECTOR *is embarrassed.*)

HECTOR	Well . . . Monday. Meet with Mr Savage without me. Get a thought or two for Birmingham in place. There's not much time. Along the lines we spoke of . . . How d'you feel about your people?
JIM	Very pleased to have Jessie Frost there. I shall get her to help me!
HECTOR	In design?
JIM	Yes. Not treading on any toes am I?
HECTOR	No, no . . .
JIM	I'm looking beyond Birmingham to the London show . . .
HECTOR	We want to see you among the awards as you were at Cauldons.
JIM	Of course, but not just me. I don't think of design any longer as a process going on inside the individual head . . . in isolation. I think of team work . . . interplay of ideas . . . many minds brought to bear . . . this is what interests me now. And if we win an award then we win it. Us. It's ours . . . collectively.

(HECTOR *is inwardly disturbed by this line of thought. It has reminded him of something.*)

HECTOR	I met someone who knows you. The local member of parliament.

JIM	(*grins*) George Maple?
HECTOR	Sir George. At the Queens Hall Ceramic Association reception. He talked about you. He said you were a fighter. He said did I realise I'd got myself a fighter? I said "good". The way things are we need a fighter. He said "that's not what I mean".

(*A pause.* HECTOR *is inviting* JIM *to comment.*)

JIM	Nothing Sir George says ever is.
HECTOR	He said he'd enjoyed crossing swords with you. I was rather taken aback.
JIM	We've sparred a bit.
HECTOR	On public platforms, he tells me.
JIM	Yes. In a small way. Politics in this ward are pretty small beer. Or they were.
HECTOR	I had no idea that you were active in that sphere . . .
JIM	We never talked about my interests, did we?
HECTOR	Well I don't pry into things when I'm interviewing. But Sir George is a particular friend and it was embarrassing not to know.
JIM	Let me tell you all about it.
HECTOR	No, no, no! Much better not to. Your opinions are your own. But we can keep them in watertight compartments. I put it this way: work is work and outside is outside . . . work. Whatever our beliefs, we can forget them when we pass the last lamp post on the way in to work and only remember them when we pass that same lamp post on the way home.

(JIM *stays quiet, deliberately making no response.*
HECTOR *changes tack as he surveys the garden.*)

How close the trees are to you here. I love the
smell of pine. Ah! You keep cats.

JIM   Mother and daughter. The mother came from the
               woods. They're almost wild.

HECTOR   (*casually*) What are they called?

               (JIM *reads his mind.*)

JIM   Sugar and Spice.

               (HECTOR *nods, privately disappointed. He was
               hoping for Lenin and Trotsky.* JIM *contains his
               irritation.* HECTOR *struggles to think of something
               to say.*)

               (*Slow fade.*)

Scene Four

*The freehand painting shop. A month later. The four paintresses
are working on Michaelmas daisies and singing an American song
of the moment. Plates awaiting removal are stacked up around
them.*

JOYCE   Are you up?

JESSIE   Nearly.

ADA   Where is he?

JOYCE   (*sings to the "Ovaltiny" radio jingle*)
               'We are the freehand painters,
               Happy girls are we!
               All day long we're decorating
               Except when Ulik keeps us waiting!"

               (*Enter* MAB *with an order.*)

MAB   He's coming. He's just up the corridor.

JOYCE   What have you got?

(MAB *quotes the order number.*)

MAB	3128 Wild Roses.
ADA	We'll be another hour on Michaelmas daisies. (*Reading the order.*) Six gross . . . that takes us through next week.

(*Enter* ULIK *with the blank ware on his trolley. He will take off the ware and stack it beside the benches on a shelf, then load the painted ware.*)

ULIK	Heyup!
JOYCE	Heyup? You mean hurry up.

(MAB *has entered the inner office to pin a copy of the order to* JIM's *workboard. He has reorganised the inner office. A number of rough designs in watercolour are pinned up or lie stacked on the desk he works at. The other desk is covered in bits and pieces, since no one uses it.*)

ADA	(*calling*) Have they altered the rates?
MAB	Not as far as I know.
JESSIE	What was it about the rates?
JOYCE	Banding! They were paying the same for banding as flowers and everyone knows there's more to flowers than banding!
MAB	Well it's still as it was.
JOYCE	I shall create over this. I shall create merry hell! It's wrong and should be put right . . . and should be put right now. And not only that, but the milk jugs were priced wrong. All the hollow ware was. You could be losing up to three shillings a week!
JESSIE	Mab . . . wasn't it decided to change the pricing?
MAB	Well if it was it never came through.

JOYCE   Ada . . .

ADA   I put it to Mr Hancock . . .

JOYCE   He'd agree to anything and forget it next day.
                 You'll have to speak to Mr Rhys.

ADA   Oh don't go on about it.

                 (MAB *whispers something to* JESSIE. ULIK *has
                 noted it with distaste. He is jealous of* MAB'S
                 friendship for his adored JESSIE.)

ULIK   (*to* JESSIE) I saw thee feyther last nate.

JESSIE   Oh didst?

ULIK   He said ter may . . . her shouldner have done it.

JESSIE   What shouldn't I have done?

ULIK   Moved away. Left them. Moved out. Left womm.

                 (*He indicates* MAB *as she exits.*)

JESSIE   You mean my father thinks I should be still paying
                 the rent so he can put his share inside him at the
                 Three Tuns.

ULIK   I dunner know about that. He wants thee back.
                 Not living with her. He said it wanner rate.

JESSIE   When I want to know what's right and what's
                 wrong, Ulik, the last person I'd ask is my father.

                 (ULIK *is downcast, wishing he hadn't spoken.*)

ULIK   Was him said it, not may.

                 (JESSIE *shuns him and returns to her bench. The
                 others, busying themselves, are aware of what's
                 going on.*)

ADA   Do we have to put up with this? The smell?

JOYCE	Did you see?
MAB	In his pocket. And half of it gone . . .
ADA	At this hour!
MAB	He'll go out of here feet first.
ADA	D'you have all your colours Jessie?

(JESSIE *doesn't answer, lost in thought about her father.*)

| VIOLET | What does it mean . . . "feet first"? |

(*Enter* JIM, *carrying an art folder.*)

JIM	Good news from Birmingham!
MAB	What? The orders?
JIM	Tell 'em.

(*He steadies his breathing.*)

MAB	Well, of the orders we took at the exhibition we've had more confirmed than we ever got last year.
ADA	Oh I am so pleased, sir!
JOYCE	We're just getting into our stride!
JIM	And so we are. A very interesting director's meeting, Miss Cooper.
MAB	Oh?
JIM	If you go and see Mr Savage you may hear something to your advantage.
MAB	About me travelling? Being made a traveller?

(JIM *just eyes her solemnly.*)

JOYCE   Go on!

MAB   (*recalling*) But . . . the designs? Jessie's designs?

JIM   Yes we discussed the designs, hers and mine.
                 Jessie put in the two tea services, "Lightning" and
                 "Saxophones". Well, they were looked at very
                 carefully . . . (*He pauses, serious faced, teasing.*)
                 And we're going ahead with saxophones!

MAB   We've done it!

JOYCE   Oh gee! Cheer up Jessie! It's not your funeral!

JIM   (*to* MAB) Go and see him. I haven't told you
                 anything.

                 (MAB *exits.* JESSIE *is thoughtful.*)

JESSIE   What about "Lightning"?

JIM   Hear that? Saxophones now. Lightning later.
                 Don't be greedy.

                 (*He goes into the inner office, getting out the
                 designs.*)

ADA   What a feather in your cap.

JOYCE   She has ideas doesn't she? I never have ideas.
                 Well . . . I have *some* ideas . . . but none that do
                 me any good. (*To* ADA.) Hey, while he's
                 smiling . . . the prices.

ADA   Yes . . .

JOYCE   Now or never . . .

                 (ADA *gets up nervously and approaches* JIM'S
                 door. As she stands a moment, JIM *suddenly
                 comes to the door and, looking past her, calls to*
                 JESSIE.)

JIM   Jessie . . . shall we go over it?

(*He nods at* ADA *and goes back into the office.*
JESSIE *crosses and joins him.* ADA *catches* JOYCE'S
eye as she is forced to sit again.)

ADA   I'll see him after . . .

VIOLET I'm always drawing musical instruments.

ADA   Let's get on, we're losing money.

JOYCE We are whether we get on or not!

     (*In the inner office* JIM *pores over* JESSIE'S
     saxophone design. He then picks up each design
     named and puts them down on the desk.)

JIM   There they were round the board room table. All
     solemn and expectant faces. I said nothing
     beyond: "These are the ones you ought to see".
     And I placed them down one by one, yours
     first . . . Lightning . . . Saxophones . . . then
     mine . . . Ocean Liner! . . . Seaplanes! . . .
     Airships! . . . Generator! . . . Pylons! If you're
     going to storm the barricades do it with all guns
     firing. There was a historic pause. Hector
     Brabant . . . not a flicker. The others . . . "ooh",
     "ah", "humm" . . . all waiting for someone else to
     break cover. Suddenly Hector speaks. "Aren't
     there any flowers?" he asks. "We always do a
     flower". I put to them the vision of the future and
     he asks, "Aren't there any flowers?" Anyway . . .
     to cut a long story short . . . we'll have to do a
     flower.

JESSIE They turned them down!

JIM   My dear Jessie they did not turn them down.
     Hector knew if he turned them down he'd see my
     heels in two seconds flat. We're doing four tea
     sets. Saxophones, Pylons, Ocean Liner . . . and a
     flower.

JESSIE I did a snowdrop pattern . . .

JIM	Oh not snowdrops! Snowdrops are sentimental. Good mind to do thistles. What about tulips? I mean tulips have a kind of strength and stridency. Could you try something?
JESSIE	I don't really know tulips . . . I don't think I've ever looked at them.
JIM	They grow in gardens.
JESSIE	We didn't have a garden . . . We had a yard.

(JIM *senses a tension behind what she's saying.*)

JIM	I'll get some and bring them in. Or some flower or other, I don't mind.
JESSIE	No, I'll do tulips.
JIM	Good. And now we have to work them all out in detail. I mean you will. I can't compete with a paintress when it comes to putting them on the ware.
JESSIE	It's normally Ada who does that.
JIM	No. You. It must be you! By the way . . . (*He picks up the Saxophone cup design.*) Putting it on the table made me look at this again. I'm not so sure about the willow leaves with the saxophones . . . they weren't in your original sketches.
JESSIE	(*firm*) They make the same shape . . . the same stroke.
JIM	Yes, I know they do . . . but . . . it's the connection that troubles me.
JESSIE	Well . . . I see the leaves like musical notes.

(JIM *brightens.*)

JIM	Then why not make them musical notes? And a more definite colour. Red?

JESSIE	You mean actual notes?
JIM	Yes.
JESSIE	Take out the willow leaves and put in notes?
JIM	Crotchets. Red crotchets.
JESSIE	But that's what I didn't want to do.
JIM	Why not?
JESSIE	Well, because it's better if the note is a willow leaf because then it's a sad note.
JIM	Why must it be sad?
JESSIE	Because saxophones are.
JIM	Saxophones are sad? D'you listen to jazz?
JESSIE	Yes . . .

(*A pause.* JESSIE *is quietly defiant.* JIM *is looking for a way forward.*)

JIM You mustn't get upset over criticism. In these times we must want things to be criticised. Working together involves an honest exchange of views. Discussion. Let's try it both ways, then we'll decide. This is a tea service, Jessie. Four o'clock tea with your crumpets and scones and cream horns. Doesn't want to be sad. It's obvious that you and I have got to discuss things more as we go along. There's so much to plan and talk about. I'd like you to move in here and use this desk.

(*He goes energetically to the other desk and clears things from it.*)

You're a designer now. And I can use your bench for a new apprentice.

JESSIE   Do I stop doing the painting?

JIM   No, we can't afford that just yet. I can pay you a
              little more. A design fee . . . and commission on
              top of your piece work. Then we'll see.

              (*He opens the door and goes into the freehand
              shop.* JESSIE *follows, still very troubled.* JIM *taps
              with a ruler and speaks.*)

              May I say something? Since Jessie will be
              working on design with me I want her to move
              into my office. Of course she'll still be doing
              painting with you. But in there. Well, that's all . . .
              oh, there was something else. There's a sale of
              work at the Co-op Assembly Rooms in aid of
              victims of silicosis in the industry. I'm sure you're
              all well aware of silicosis . . . .and the criminal
              neglect of the sufferers. I hope you'll be able to
              go . . .

              (JESSIE *burns with anger at his brusque handling
              of her situation. Suddenly she exits. A pause as*
              JIM *falters, uncertainly, then collects himself and
              carries on.*)

              Thousands die of it. I expect you all know
              someone who has. And without proper extractors
              to get the flint dust out of the air, more will. Some
              of them working across that yard right now. You
              may as well fill your lungs with broken glass. We
              talk of the beauty of the products of the potteries.
              Where's the beauty in that? They won't need
              beauty in the pot they spit their life into. So we
              need to support the fighting fund for prevention
              and compensation and care - not just for silicosis
              but all industrial disease - and I say: all disease,
              full stop! Beauty? Beauty? You can take the
              works of Shakespeare and I'll add Flaubert and
              Tolstoy. You can take Beethoven's Pastoral and
              Elgar's Violin Concerto. You can take the ceiling
              of the Sistine Chapel . . . put them all together and
              throw in the Cathedral at Chartres, and you still
              won't have the beauty of a nation that simply,

freely and gladly cares for its sick. I'm sorry.
There it is . . .

(*He glances towards the exit, wishing* JESSIE *would
return, then exits to his office.*)

ADA   She's going to work in with him!

JOYCE   Well of course she is!

ADA   Where's she gone? Where did she go to?

           (JOYCE *realises why* JESSIE *left so angrily. She
           "covers".*)

JOYCE   Where d'you think she's gone to? We can still
           spend a penny when we want can't we?

ADA   What has he done? Nothing was said.

JOYCE   It was. He's just told us.

ADA   I mean to me!

VIOLET   Can I have her place?

           (*The dinner break hooter goes.* JIM, *who has
           been slumped at his desk, deep in thought, now
           grabs his jacket and takes off his overall.* JOYCE
           indicates him to ADA.)

JOYCE   Catch him! Talk about the price for these!

ADA   Oh! Erm . . .

           (*But as* JIM *walks through the freehand shop* ADA
           is too disheartened to speak. JOYCE *senses it.*)

JOYCE   Well look it's sort of sunny. The first sun we've
           seen this year. Let's sit on the wall and eat our
           snappin. It's been a long winter . . .

ADA   Yes.

(They get their sandwich boxes and tea cans and go. VIOLET *has buried herself in her work, not wanting to be asked. As soon as they exit she crosses to* JESSIE'S *desk and examines the saxophone design. From her bag she takes a sketch book and out of it some design sketches of her own. She compares them. Her eye turns to* JIM'S *office. Listening for anyone coming, she crosses with her sketches and, entering the inner office, compares them with* JIM'S *designs.* ULIK *now enters bringing some ware.* VIOLET *hides herself.* ULIK *looks at* JESSIE'S *designs with contempt. He is still disturbed by their last encounter. He sits and takes from one pocket a small medicine bottle full of milk and from the other a chemist's bottle of methylated spirits, purple-blue. In a slightly ritualistic way he takes a drink of milk, followed by a mouthful of meths, holding his mouth and nose as he swallows to hold it down.* VIOLET *peers out at him. He looks straight ahead and speaks without turning his head.)*

ULIK   *(seeing her reflected in a window)* I can see thee. I can see thee. What at doin in theer?

                (He turns to her. She comes out.)

                I could see thee reflection in the winder pane. Hasner sane anyone drinking the blue before?

                (He takes another pull of milk, chased by a mouthful of meths and holds it down. She stares in fear and fascination. He very nearly vomits . . . threatening JESSIE'S *designs.)*

VIOLET   Don't do that! Those are designs.

ULIK   Designs? Designs? They're not designs. They're daubings. Daubings, not designs! Slapped on! Daubed on! I could do better painting with a donkey's teel!

                (He scatters the designs violently. VIOLET *eyes him with contempt and exits swiftly to warn*

someone. ULIK *now relents. Picks up the fallen
designs shakily and murmurs over them.*)

Her shouldner do it. Her shouldner be axed ter
do it. Her shouldner do such things.

(*The lights fade.*)

Scene Five

MAB *and* JESSIE'S *flat above a shop, by a tram route in town.* MAB
*sits by the gas fire in her slip, staring into the glow, dreaming. She
has a travelling clock held close to her ear.* JESSIE *is stretching a
canvass over a frame. She works on their small dining table,
covered in newspaper.*

MAB   I love my little travelling clock, d'you know? I
               like the way it sits up and the way it folds flat and
               the way it smells of Morocco. It's got a naggy little
               tick that keeps you on the mark . . . getatit, getatit,
               getatit! And when it rings you've got to stop it
               quick or it judders itself off the table.

JESSIE   I shan't miss it.

MAB   It was one of the first things I ever bought myself,
               except for food and clothes. From Lewis's in
               Manchester. I like getting small items from big
               places. They had this advertisement that said: "Put
               time in your suitcase."

               (JESSIE *offers her a sweet.*)

               Shall you think of me in Leeds?

JESSIE   Coping with your gentlemen?

MAB   Yes. I shall come back deaf. I thought you were
               loud enough in the Potteries till I went to Leeds.
               D'you suppose Jim Rhys had anything to do with
               it?

JESSIE   Why would he?

MAB   He gave you a leg up. But then he doesn't like
             me does he?

JESSIE   Why shouldn't he?

MAB   What d'you think of him?

JESSIE   I think he's so driven. Always has to be on the
             attack. He can't let something just happen.

MAB   I meant as a man.

JESSIE   Oh . . . I'm not going to comment on that. I had
             more than enough of that at art school as you well
             know. I thought: I'm not going to be standoffish
             and snotty. I'm not going to be one of those hard
             and haughty types with their crushing remarks
             and insults. I'm going to be pleasant to men. What
             a mistake that was!

MAB   Jessie, when there's five of us women standing in
             the freehand shop, as far as he's concerned
             there's just you.

JESSIE   Hm! He disappointed me the way he did nothing
             when Ulik was sacked.

MAB   Ulik doesn't come under him.

JESSIE   Believing as he does he should have done
             something.

MAB   Oh Jessie! Ulik should have been sacked months
             ago. Hector only kept him on because he'd been
             in the navy! He was sleeping on the premises at
             night . . . by the kilns!

JESSIE   He has nowhere.

MAB   Suppose he'd got the fireman drunk and we'd lost
             a kiln full of ware. There'd have been more
             people sacked than him! He was also a thief.
             Took ware and sold it for drink . . . and it was
             your drawings he messed up!

JESSIE	He only spilled milk on them.
MAB	Milk? He was drinking methylated spirits!
JESSIE	He has it with milk.
MAB	How foul!
JESSIE	He has to have the milk to keep it down. Don't you know?
MAB	What is it you've got about that man?

(JESSIE *smiles and shakes her head*.)

He loves being what he is you know. He thinks he's celebrated. Doesn't wash. Smells rancid. Lice, I shouldn't wonder. You have such fine things to do! If he's got any hold on you, he'll use it. You hear me? You're a designer now!

JESSIE	If I was allowed to design.
MAB	You can't have everything your own way . . .
JESSIE	Well then how are they mine if they're not my own way? Red notes with the saxophones? What can I do?
MAB	Argue with him! I did with Savage.
JESSIE	You can. I can't. Arguments get lost in my head. And if I argued he'd argue better. He has to be right. Oh I was stirred up by him when he first came but he turns out to be just another of these men who have to be right.
MAB	We all think we're right.
JESSIE	And so we should about what's ours. He wants to be right about what's mine!

(MAB *decides not to press further. She consults the paper on the table*.)

MAB   What shall we see? There's Ronald Coleman at
                the Roxy . . . but I have no time at all for that little
                moustache. There's a Garbo . . . I don't know. I'd
                go like a shot to a Bette Davis and where is she?

                (*A faint knock on door downstairs.*)

                Was that ours?

JESSIE   Yes.

MAB   I'll see what he's selling. The way I feel I'd even
                buy a brush.

                (*She exits, pulling on her dress.* JESSIE *is quite still
                for a moment or two, then takes another canvas
                with a landscape painted on it. She inspects it,
                carefully. Enter* MAB.)

MAB   It's Grace Rhys . . . Mrs Rhys! D'you know her?

JESSIE   No . . .

MAB   She's broken her heel . . . (*Turns back to the
                door.*) Please come in. Enter our marble halls!

                (*Enter* GRACE, *one shoe in hand.*)

GRACE   I'll have to hobble, I'm afraid. How d'you do? I
                do feel a twerp! And are you Jessie Frost? How
                funny meeting like this. Wonderful! That's Jim's
                word for you . . . "Wonderful". He says you are
                doing wonderful things.

MAB   (*to* JESSIE) Well, there you are . . .

JESSIE   Not wonderful . . .

GRACE   That's what he says. Actually I've met you but
                you wouldn't know it . . . D'you remember Bunty
                Wooliscroft?

JESSIE   Er . . .

GRACE   She used to go around with Sheila Leak. Your
           cousin.

JESSIE   No . . . the only female cousin I have is Jean
           Phillips.

           (GRACE *makes a show of searching her mind.*)

GRACE   That's who I mean! Jean! We were in town one
           day and she pointed out your door. So when this
           happened I thought, I'll see if they're in

MAB   Where did you do it?

GRACE   Thursday.

           (*They look puzzled.*)

           What am I talking about? Thursday? I mean in
           front of Woolworth's. The grid in the footpath. I
           felt such a chump! Such a tripehound! Wobbling
           along like little dot and carry one!

MAB   Well we can just about offer you a chair if Jessie
           hasn't left her brushes or paint on it.

GRACE   Oh you are a fearless pair you two, having a flat!

JESSIE   Are we?

GRACE   To be free and have the world rushing past your
           window. It's such a back water where we are
           you'd think life had gone away for ever. Oh I
           feel that every girl should have a year or two of
           pleasing herself these days. Then at least you'd
           always know what it was you'd given up.

           (MAB *has been examining the shoe.*)

MAB   I think this'll go back on.

JESSIE   I'll get my hammer . . .

GRACE   Are you going to do it?

MAB   They do it deliberately. They make them weak to
               make work for cobblers. I use the back of the flat
               iron.

               (*She gets an old fashioned flat iron, puts it on the
               table and slips the shoe over the handle.*)

               (*to* JESSIE) Move your picture!

JESSIE   Line it up properly . . .

MAB   Don't tell me what to do . . .

JESSIE   I've got a longer nail. It was sticking out of the
               back of the kitchen dresser.

MAB   You'll pull the house down.

               (*She takes the nail and tries to push it into the
               leather.*)

JESSIE   Use the scissors . . .

               (JESSIE *makes a hole for the nail with the point of
               the scissor blade. All this time* GRACE *takes in the
               pair of them, living so easily together. The heel is
               mended.*)

MAB   What about that?

GRACE   And I thought it'd need a man to do it.

MAB   A man, Mrs Rhys? A man? The more I think of
               men the more I love my dog.

GRACE   Have you got a dog?

JESSIE   No we haven't.

GRACE   I have. I don't love him a lot, though. Well!
               Thank you very much. Oh it must be famous just
               being the two of you here . . . doing everything
               yourselves.

(GRACE *walks a step or two gingerly.*)

JESSIE It'll see you home . . .

(*An awkward moment.* JESSIE *is aware of* GRACE'S *possible jealousy.* MAB *is suspicious about her intentions.* GRACE *picks up the painting.*)

GRACE You never did this, did you?

MAB She did.

GRACE I didn't know you did paintings.

JESSIE I do landscapes.

GRACE Jim never said.

JESSIE He'd have seen some of mine at Burslem Art School.

(GRACE *senses the implied criticism.*)

GRACE (*to* MAB) She mustn't let him bully her.

MAB I've been saying.

GRACE He'll always overbear you if he can. It doesn't much matter in my case 'cos I've got no brains. None at all. It's been decided. I don't read the right books and if I did I wouldn't have anything to say about them . . . (*Changes subject, inspecting the painting.*) I do like those trees.

JESSIE They're beeches . . . beyond Trentham, on the hill.

GRACE I like the way they stand in a circle.

JESSIE It's just how they were . . . though I've made more of it. Like a circle of giants!

MAB She never does anything but trees . . .

JESSIE   The first I really got interested in were some ash trees in Shropshire, where we got taken from art school. They were huge! Till then I'd only ever been out of Burslem to the moors where you get more sky than trees. Well, and there was this old fellow . . . this village fellow talking while I was sketching. He called them "creatures". Creatures! I'd never thought of a tree being called a creature . . . But it should be so . . .

MAB   She's tree mad, I'm afraid.

GRACE   I wish I was madder. If I'm what you call sane where's it got me?

JESSIE   . . . Because they shouldn't be painted as objects. Their lives may be much longer than ours but they're lives. One day they won't be there. Like we won't. And its all very well saying trees are beautiful . . . as though that was the only point. Beauty has to struggle like anything else.

(GRACE *is struck by this, applying it to herself. She smiles at* JESSIE. MAB *feels uncomfortable.*)

MAB   She had two paintings in the North Staffs Artists Exhibition you know . . .

GRACE   Did you really?

JESSIE   They took them rather grudgingly because my teacher had got at them . . . and they hung them in a side bit where not many people saw them.

GRACE   Could I see them?

JESSIE   Oh. They've been taken. My aunt Emma has them. I have this wonderful aunt who lives in Derbyshire, in Matlock Spa. She's widowed and she keeps a shop . . . a souvenir shop. She's a real go-getter and was outraged when no one bought my paintings at the Exhibition. She took them off to sell in her window. I went over and saw them there in amongst the jugs and ewers and

	cheese dishes saying: "Welcome to Matlock". It killed me! I did laugh!
GRACE	And did anyone buy them?
JESSIE	No! I'm still waiting!
GRACE	Could I? That one.
JESSIE	What?
GRACE	Buy it.
JESSIE	Oh no. I'll give it you.
GRACE	No . . .
JESSIE	I must. I'll put something round it.

(*She wraps brown paper around it and ties it with string.*)

GRACE	I shall think of something to give you in exchange.

(*Again,* MAB *is discomforted by the bond the two have set up.*)

MAB	She has a passion for Licorice Allsorts . . .
JESSIE	Will you stay?
GRACE	No. No. Jim's expecting me back and I'm overdue now. We're going to a meeting. (*Waves her foot.*) This feels as good as new.
MAB	Have you got far to walk?
GRACE	The car's just up the street. By the Town Hall.
MAB	Car? You drive a car?
GRACE	I have to, living out there.

MAB   A car of your own?

GRACE   Yes. A little Ford. Jim has a Lancia.

MAB   Two cars!!

JESSIE   It's her dream to own a car!

MAB   Was it hard learning? To drive?

GRACE   No! Not if you don't mind letting yourself go,
               launching off, and trusting yourself to fate! Mind
               you, being able to drive means I'm nothing but a
               chauffeur half the time. Today I've been loaded
               up with things for the party.

MAB   You're having a party?

GRACE   (*wishing she hadn't said it*) Oh no. I mean the
               Labour Party. Well. I'm glad I came to see you.
               You'd perhaps like to come and look at our pines.
               We have a pine plantation at the end of the
               garden.

JESSIE   Pines . . . Yes. Yes, I would.

GRACE   Well . . . bye, bye.

               (MAB *sees her down the flight of stairs to the
               street door.*)

MAB   (*off*) You'll know where to come next time.

GRACE   (*off*) I mustn't make a habit of it, must I?

MAB   (*off*) Bye, bye.

GRACE   (*off*) Thank you so much.

               (MAB *returns.*)

MAB   The Labour Party!

JESSIE   She's not very good at hiding things. Didn't you see in her bag?

MAB   What?

JESSIE   She'd covered them with her library books but I could see a toe sticking out. She had another pair of shoes!

(MAB *realises. They begin to see the funny side of it. The lights fade.*)

Scene Six

The garden of the Pines. JIM *is working at the garden table, making notes on sketches in a sketch block. He has a blanket wrapped around him. A wind up gramophone is beside him playing the final movement theme from the second symphony of Sibelius.* HECTOR *appears in shooting clothes, carrying a shot gun. It is a keen, crisp April morning.* HECTOR *lets the music finish.* JIM *wipes his eyes.*

HECTOR   Good morning!

JIM   Caught me! He always sweeps me away. (*Referring to Sibelius.*) You only have to hear him to know that something's afoot. Something's astir.

HECTOR   (*noting the blanket*) Aren't you well?

JIM   Fine. Just cold working out here but I like the air. This year's full of false starts.

HECTOR   A reluctant spring. Well I'd prefer it gustier and colder for wood pigeons. Let them ride the wind. But I think the sun's on his way now. Are you sure you won't join me? I've cleaned and oiled the Baretta. It's in the car if you want it. I've plenty of ammunition.

JIM   I'd only show off my clumsiness. A six gun's more my style.

HECTOR   I really am very grateful, Jim . . . you letting me
            get amongst your feathered fraternity.

JIM   They're not mine . . . I don't own the place, you
            know. No. I rent. I don't own.

HECTOR   You don't own the house?

JIM   No.

            (HECTOR *suspects a political point and lets it pass.
            Enter from the house,* GRACE *and* JESSIE *with trays
            of tea things.*)

HECTOR   Grace. Shall you have the birds to make a pie?

GRACE   I thought you were going to shoot rabbits . . .

HECTOR   If I see a bunny and you want it I shall . . . but it's
            the poor man's partridge I'm here for.

GRACE   Oh shoot what you like. Shoot anything. Shoot
            everything! Shoot 'em all! There's been so much
            messing and marauding and pulling up what you
            plant it's time we had some revenge. Oh, it's an
            endless struggle of birds and animals and people
            round here.

            (*This seems to be aimed vaguely at* JIM. *There is
            an embarrassed pause.* HECTOR *tries a joke.*)

HECTOR   Well I'm not here to shoot people.

JIM   Have you noticed what they've brought? It's the
            new designs. There's a cup and a plate from each
            of the sample sets. I thought we might christen
            them.

JESSIE   Pylons . . . Ocean Liner . . . Tulips and
            Saxophones.

            (*She indicates each cup.* HECTOR *examines them.*)

HECTOR	(*examining cups*) Now I've seen you . . . and you . . . (*With Saxophones.*) Ah . . . was this like this? These musical notes with the saxophones?
JIM	(*briskly*) We're considering that one still. As an alternative.
HECTOR	(*to* JESSIE) What was there before?
JESSIE	(*glancing at* JIM) Willow leaves.
HECTOR	Ah yes . . .

(*He has a preference for the willow leaves but he decides not to get involved.*)

Well, we're ready for the London show, I believe.

GRACE	Shall I be shouted at if I pour tea in them? (*She does so.*) I never dare use samples. They stay wrapped up in their boxes and never come out. Years later you open the box and find one and you think: did we suffer sleepless nights for that? It's funny, putting yourself on the rack for a cup and saucer.
HECTOR	(*uncomfortable*) Ah! Women must weep!
GRACE	Weep? I don't weep.
HECTOR	I meant it . . . poetically.
GRACE	I don't see any poetry in weeping.
JIM	(*irritated with her*) What cake is it?
GRACE	How should I know?
JIM	You made it.
GRACE	I didn't. It was delivered. It could be anything. Coconut, I expect. I asked for Madeira.

JIM   It is Madeira.

                    (HECTOR *changes the subject.*)

HECTOR   (*raising his cup to* JESSIE) Tulips has come out
                    awfully well. Congratulations.

JESSIE   (*holding back her irritation*) Thank you . . .

HECTOR   I do like a good flower. So do the public. And
                    Saxophones is very jolly . . . and Ocean Liner . . .

                    (*He is mindful of* JIM *as designer, but his distaste
                    comes through slightly on the last.*)

                    . . . and Pylons.

GRACE   Pylons are awful things! They've plonked one
                    right in the middle of the fields we used to play in.

JIM   Nonsense! They bring us light, heat,
                    telephones . . . especially telephones. People
                    speaking to people. Only the few as yet but more
                    and more to come . . . spreading news . . .
                    organising . . . spreading ideas . . .

HECTOR   (*quickly*) Has Jim told you you're coming to
                    London, Jessie? We shall want you there in case
                    you win a prize . . . (*Corrects himself.*) *We* win a
                    prize.

JESSIE   I've hardly been out of the Potteries!

HECTOR   Oh Miss Frost! Miss Jessica Frost! There is a
                    world beyond the bottle kilns!

                    (*He finishes his tea and shoulders his gun and
                    tackle.*)

                    I'll walk through the fir plantation and get to the
                    old wood before I start shooting. I'll see you in an
                    hour.

                    (*He salutes and exits to the wood.*)

JIM	Oh the effort of being polite!
JESSIE	Were you being polite?
GRACE	Didn't you notice? (*She remembers something.*) Oh! The dog's loose! I must get him in before the shooting starts! Marx! Marx!

(*She rushes off to the house.*)

JESSIE	This is the first garden I've ever been in.
JIM	Oh yes. You had a yard.
JESSIE	I've been to the gates of gardens but never right in.
JIM	You know we have your painting hung in the house?
JESSIE	She told me.
JIM	I'm very impressed. Grace loves it. You obviously intend more than just trees. It's good to be a Sunday painter. Some of the greatest were Sunday painters. Douanier Rousseau, the French customs man. He painted trees.
JESSIE	Yes, but he painted his with tigers. I could paint your pines with the cats.
JIM	Now that's a good idea. Pines! Here they've been on my doorstep and I've never used them. They'd make a good design. They're not English. They have a sense of far off countries to me . . . of Norway and Russia. I have a daydream that the future will come marching out from them with bands playing and banners flying . . . Oh do your painting but do it as a design as well.

(*She looks suddenly towards the wood.*)

JESSIE	I'm wondering when he's going to shoot. D'you agree with him killing birds?

JIM   They're vermin. They'd eat all the crops if they
                weren't kept down. I've shot them myself before
                now. It's his turnout that I find ridiculous . . .
                making some field sports ritual out of it. Wood
                pigeons are working class!

JESSIE   Then why aren't you defending them?

JIM   Because they're thieves, opportunists and
                hooligans. They lack a sense of social purpose
                and responsibility. Not all the class are worth
                saving, Jessie.

JESSIE   So put me with the ones that aren't.

                (*He looks at her intently.*)

JIM   You're not going to budge from this are you?

JESSIE   How d'you mean?

JIM   You'll stay with me. You'll stick with the job? See
                it through?

JESSIE   Of course!

JIM   There's no "of course" in anything. You make a
                decision. I want you to say it.

JESSIE   What? Say what?

JIM   I'll get you some more money when I can. D'you
                think you're badly paid?

JESSIE   No. Everyone thinks I've done well. Mab and I
                are planning to go shares in a gramophone.

JIM   Does *she* think you've done well?

JESSIE   Yes. What are you wanting me to say?

JIM   If you get any offers elsewhere come and tell me.
                Tell me before you decide anything. Won't you?

JESSIE   Why d'you search me like this?

JIM   I have to know that you're with me . . . or it'd be no use.

                (*He reaches for her hand.*)

                Jessie, if two people form a partnership - I'm giving you a warning now - if two people come together and make something successful of it, there are those in this world who won't be able to rest until they've driven a wedge in. We must resist that. We must act together, support one another and make sure our bond can't be broken. Because they'll try.

JESSIE   Who will?

                (*She wonders if he means* GRACE. *He realises and deflects this.*)

JIM   Hector and his clan. Oh yes . . . if we're too successful. Their style is to divide. You promise?

JESSIE   I'm not sure what it is you're trying to make me promise.

                (*He pretends it's been a joke. He offers her the saxophone cup and saucer.*)

JIM   I'll make you swear it on your work.

                (*A shot distantly. The dog barks indoors.*)

GRACE   (*off*) Has he started?

JIM   (*to himself*) No, he's finished. They're all finished. They've all outlived their time.

                (*Another shot.*)

JESSIE   Oh whatever is he killing them for?

JIM   There's no room for their dull minds in our
                   scheme of things, Jessie. This is not their world
                   any more. Their world's dead and they should be
                   gone! That's the task for us two. You understand
                   me? Together . . .

                   (GRACE *comes from the house and immediately*
                   senses the mood between them.)

GRACE   Jessie! . . . There's Leese's taxi cab at the gate
                   with Mab Cooper getting out of it.

JESSIE   (*delighted*) She's here already?

GRACE   She's come early!

JESSIE   (*calls*) Mab!

                   (JIM *is furious at the interruption. Enter* MAB. *The*
                   sound of the cab is heard driving away.)

MAB   Jessie! I took an earlier train than I said I would.
                   Good morning Mr Rhys.

JIM   Good morning. Have some tea? Excuse me, I
                   need something.

                   (*He exits to the house.*)

MAB   What have I interrupted?

GRACE   I don't know.

JESSIE   How was Leeds?

MAB   Well, I didn't fall flat on my face . . . and I got one
                   new order. It was wonderful really.

GRACE   What about you being a woman?

MAB   A one minute wonder. I think they enjoy the
                   novelty. They'd almost all met me before when I
                   did the rounds with Mr Eardsley. Mind you, I

think I do better being female . . . they increase their orders just to show off! And I did get half a proposal.

JESSIE   Who from?

MAB   The buyer at Protheroe's in Halifax. He said if I could get him another five percent discount he'd lead me to the altar.

GRACE   Don't let them cheek you!

MAB   I simply said if we lowered the discount I'd get less commission so I would need to know first whether he was able to compensate me for that. He went red as the setting sun!

(Two more shots, distantly.)

JESSIE   It's Hector Brabant, shooting birds . . .

MAB   Not really?

GRACE   We shall have Jim shooting next! He's gone for his gun . . . I know he has.

JESSIE   He has a gun?

GRACE   Not a shotgun. A what-d'you call it . . . like a cowboy's.

MAB   A revolver.

GRACE   Yes. Oh he loves it. He sleeps with it under his pillow.

JESSIE   Why?

GRACE   He says it's in case the revolution starts in the middle of the night. *(Calls.)* Jim! Don't let Marx out! I've shut him in the cellar!

(JIM enters from the house with a Colt 38 service revolver.)

JIM   There are boss guns and there are anti-boss
               guns. Worker's guns!

MAB   Is that real?

GRACE   Yes. And it's not a worker's gun, it's an officer's
               gun.

JIM   It depends what use you put it to. Shall we part
               Hector's hair?

GRACE   Don't talk like that in front of Mab and Jessie!

JIM   Maybe they'd like to fire the first shot . . .

GRACE   He won't let me touch it. He's afraid I'd point it at
               him!

JIM   Come on Jessie. Defend your proletarian
               pigeons. Come on, Mab. You've told me you're
               from the slums of Manchester. Fire the opening
               shot in the class war.

MAB   If you provoke me I'll tell you what I think of
               remarks like that . . .

JIM   Hello! It's gone quiet. What's he doing in there?
               Has he shot his fill already? Is it all too much for
               him d'you think? Are the feathered corpses
               hanging in scores from the trees? Too much
               blood spattered on the bark? Oh wonderful to say
               you've had enough when you already have too
               much.

JESSIE   Point it in the air!

JIM   He's half a mile away! There's a hundred tree
               trunks between us. A maze of blockheaded,
               stupid, futile argument! How can a bullet ever find
               it's way through that!

               (*A shot, distant.*)

JESSIE   Don't!

| JIM | It has to be answered! |
| | |

(*He shoots into the wood.*)

| JESSIE | Stop! |

| MAB | There's someone there . . . |

| GRACE | Someone's fallen! |

| JESSIE | By that bush . . . |

| JIM | It can't be him . . . |

| JESSIE | It isn't. It's Ulik. (*Quietly.*) I knew he'd be somewhere. |

(ULIK *staggers from the wood, wet through. He's on the meths, laughing at the shooting.*)

| ULIK | Battle stations! All hands! Fire! What's wrong with our bloody ships? (*Does a posh voice.*) What's wrong with our bloody ships . . . the admiral says! Fire! |

(*He stumbles, falling to his knees.* JESSIE *rushes to him. The others, frozen for a moment, follow.*)

| JESSIE | Are you hit? Are you shot? |

| ULIK | Oh I'm bulletproof when I'm on the blue! |

(ULIK *draws out his bottle of meths.*)

This keeps out the bullets! Yea, though I walk in the valley of the shadow of death!

| JIM | He's not hurt . . . |

| JESSIE | He is! |

| ULIK | (*to his bottle*) For thou art with me . . . |

| JIM | He wasn't even in the firing line. |

MAB   Oh, look at his shirt!

               (*She pulls back, disgusted.*)

ULIK   Thou comforts me . . .

JESSIE   You're sopping wet. Have you been out all night?

ULIK   Why should I care about the rain? Why fear the
               black cloud's stormy thunder? Wherever I go I
               have my own little bit of blue . . . for I was one of
               the boys in blue . . . sailing the ocean main!

GRACE   Jim! Can't you say something? This is our garden!

               (ULIK *stoops and bows to* JIM.)

ULIK   Mr Rhys, sir. I've served King and country. Set
               me on my way with a shilling sir.

               (*He lurches against* JIM *who is angered by this
               abasement.*)

JIM   Stand up . . . stand up! I'll give you a shilling . . .

JESSIE   Wait!

               (*She runs to the garden chair to get her purse
               from her bag. She pushes money into* ULIK's
               hand. ULIK *sobers and becomes more dignified.*
               JIM *is transfixed by* JESSIE's *sudden urgency.*)

ULIK   Oh see this wench? Oh see this woman . . . as I
               have known from a child and watched her grow
               in goodness. Her's so kind . . . as though all the
               kindness that lacks in others should be put in one
               young heart. Her's too kind . . . too soft, sir, for
               her own good. Her's too ready to be swayed.
               You see sir . . . her can paint . . . no sir, I mean
               "paint" . . . not daubing . . . not slapping it on. I
               mean her could paint the air, the sky! Rivers that
               flow . . . trees where shadows sway. The quick
               kingfisher in the stream, her'd catch it with her
               brush! Her can paint the daylight all around! Her

could paint the stars so that if they ever fell to earth and none of us knew where they'd once been . . . her'd know, and show us how they once did shine! Her shouldn't be asked to do what her's asked to do, sir. That lowers her. It's beneath her. Oh I love her this side of God Almighty, for there's nothing in His creation her can't paint . . .

(JIM *sees how* JESSIE *is held in* ULIK'S *spell*. MAB *can't understand* JESSIE'S *bond with the man.* GRACE *senses her husband's anguish and fear that he will lose* JESSIE'S *strength*.)

(*The lights fade. End of Act One.*)

ACT TWO

Scene One

The freehand paint shop, after hours. VIOLET has remained to work on some of her own design sketches that she doesn't want others to see. Enter RAYMOND PARKER, here to be interviewed for the new apprenticeship. VIOLET is annoyed. She will instinctively cover her work.

VIOLET	You're in the wrong place.
RAYMOND	I was told.
VIOLET	Told what?
RAYMOND	To come up here. To see the art director.
VIOLET	Who?
RAYMOND	Mr Rhys.
VIOLET	Who told you?
RAYMOND	A woman.
VIOLET	She shouldn't have. There's valuable ware in here and there might have been no one. No one's supposed to enter . . . unless they're with somebody. Sit by that bench but don't touch anything.

(A silence. VIOLET enjoys his discomfort.)

RAYMOND	Is this the freehand shop?
VIOLET	What's it look like? Are you after the job?

(He nods.)

RAYMOND	Freehand apprentice.
VIOLET	You?

RAYMOND   Yes.

VIOLET   Done your classes?

RAYMOND   Evening classes . . .

VIOLET   Where?

RAYMOND   Hanley.

               (VIOLET *sniffs*.)

VIOLET   Is this the first job you've gone after?

RAYMOND   No.

VIOLET   How many have you been turned down for?

RAYMOND   Four. (*Pause*.) Five.

VIOLET   I suppose you know it's only women in here?

               (RAYMOND *doesn't know what to say*.)

               Didn't you know? Didn't they tell you? It's
               freehand painting so it's bound to be women. Men
               aren't quick enough at it. Boys aren't. It's in the
               fingers. Women have the fingers. Men don't. It's
               well known . . . women can keep up . . . men
               can't. I mean when you get off your apprentice
               pay and onto piecework you'd never be able to
               keep up. You wouldn't make your money. That's
               why you don't see men doing it. They can't.
               They're not able to.

               (*She pretends to finish off a sketch while
               RAYMOND nurses his feelings of fear and
               hopelessness. After a little while she puts the
               drawings away and collects her things for home.
               RAYMOND rises as she crosses to the door*.)

RAYMOND   Shall I? . . .

VIOLET   Shall you what? Sit there and I'll see if there's
                  anyone around. I'm not going to stay all night.

                  (*As she is about to exit* JESSIE *enters.*)

JESSIE   Are you Raymond Parker?

VIOLET   He wants to be taken on.

JESSIE   Mr Rhys won't be long.

VIOLET   Apprentice freehand painting.

                  (JESSIE *reacts to the implied offensiveness in her
                  tone.* VIOLET *exits.* JESSIE *allows a little pause.*)

JESSIE   Goodnight Violet. (*Then to* RAYMOND.) You're
                  here on your own?

RAYMOND   My father works late but he'll come if you want a
                  paper signing.

JESSIE   Have a square of chocolate?

                  (*She offers one from the packet. They both
                  munch quietly a moment.*)

RAYMOND   Thank you miss. Is it true you only take on girls?

JESSIE   What?

RAYMOND   As apprentices?

JESSIE   Who said that?

                  (*He doesn't answer. She guesses.*)

                  You wouldn't have been asked to come if we only
                  took on girls. (*Listens.*) That's him. Look him in
                  the eye. He likes you to look him straight in the
                  eye.

                  (*Enter* JIM.)

JIM   Now Raymond Parker . . . What makes you think
you've got it in you to be the best freehand
painter in the Potteries?

(RAYMOND *grins*.)

We'll have a look at what you've brought shall
we?

(JESSIE *is about to leave*.)

Can you stay Jessie? While we see his work. This
is Jessie Frost.

RAYMOND   I saw her photo with you in the Pottery and Glass
Record. Winning the prize for the tea sets in
London.

(RAYMOND *has opened out his art folder and
while* JIM *glances through he unwraps a
decorated vase from a cardboard box in his bag*.)

JIM   And you read about us?

RAYMOND   Yes sir. And in the Sentinel.

JIM   I'm looking for content, Raymond. It's not just
whether you can make strokes. D'you know what
I mean? I'm looking for your thoughts. How you
want others to think when they see what you've
done . . .

(JESSIE *has examined the vase and passes it to*
JIM.)

What d'you want your patterns to mean to
people?

RAYMOND   Something they like looking at . . .

JIM   "Like". Yes . . . but what should they think?

RAYMOND   That it's well done.

JIM   What d'you feel about modern design?

RAYMOND   I've done some modern at the back. There's a
             "Wireless" one. I thought, people having tea
             listening to the wireless. And this one's roller
             skating . . .

             (JIM *is pleased and glances at* JESSIE.)

JIM   Like to ask anything?

             (JESSIE *picks up the vase.*)

JESSIE   How'd you get this green?

RAYMOND   I put a Ramsden's Cobalt to an Emery's Yellow.
             The numbers are on the bottom.

             (JESSIE *turns the vase over.* JIM *can see she likes
             the boy. He takes out a letter.*)

JIM   You know I've got a letter from your teacher, Mr
             Henderson. Raymond's a swimmer, Jessie. Won
             the inter-schools backstroke. Well Mr Henderson
             thinks you're alright. I'll speak to your father.

JESSIE   He's not here. He works late.

JIM   I'll give you a note for him. What d'you say
             Jessie?

JESSIE   Oh, I agree!

             (JIM *finds a pad and scribbles a note.* JESSIE *smiles
             encouragingly.*)

JIM   This asks him to allow you to have the usual trial
             and if he'd like to pop in and see me . . .

             (*He puts the note in an envelope and seals it.*)

             Monday morning at eight thirty. Here.

RAYMOND   Right! Thank you! Thank you!

JIM Jessie will show you what to do.

RAYMOND Goodnight.

JIM Goodnight Master Parker.

(RAYMOND *exits.* JIM *makes a note.*)

JIM He's the one.

JESSIE How chancy our beginnings are, the way we blow down one path rather than another . . . get shown a door that opens to us and because it opens we go through.

(JIM, *writing in the inner office, does not really hear.*)

JIM He seemed a straight sort of lad. Looks you in the eye. And he's for others. (*In answer to her enquiring glance.*) I divide people into two kinds according to whether they seem to be more for others or themselves. It's the most fundamental question. Will he put his talents at the service of the team or himself?

(JESSIE *becomes guarded. Not to be drawn on this issue. He changes the mood.*)

Shall we look at "Pines"?

(*He finds the sketches on her desk.*)

Putting in the lightning flash is very clever.

JESSIE Well they turned down lightning on its own so I thought I'll use it in "Pines".

JIM The same zig-zag. The same stroke as the branches.

JESSIE Like willow leaves and saxophones.

(JIM *grins. Then ponders.*)

JIM   One thing . . . should the pines slope away from the lightning . . . not towards?

JESSIE   Away.

JIM   Why?

JESSIE   Because that's how I saw it.

JIM   You must have your reasons.

JESSIE   You never like my reasons.

JIM   Can't say if I don't know what they are.

JESSIE   I'd prefer it judged without reasons.

(JIM *scrutinises the design again.*)

JIM   Alright. To me it throws the design more off balance. But then . . . that's good. We want to throw people off balance . . .

JESSIE   You do.

JIM   Fight me! If you think I'm wrong, fight me! But fight me with arguments. You take up an emotional position before everything's discussed! We have to be open to one another.

(*His tone has softened. She tenses.*)

JESSIE   That's too dangerous for me. I'm too easily swayed.

JIM   I remember those words. Ulik . . .

JESSIE   Ulik? Remember is right. He's dead.

JIM   No . . .

JESSIE   Pneumonia. He was found in a field by some children. Well, their dog found him.

(JIM *is genuinely shocked.*)

JIM   He was bound to destroy himself, Jessie.

JESSIE   He was no good at discussion.

JIM   When did it happen?

JESSIE   While I was in London being famous!

JIM   You weren't his keeper.

JESSIE   No one was.

(*A pause.* JIM *thinks hard before speaking.*)

JIM   Why is it all the time I feel you slipping and sliding away? We're the twin souls of this town Jessie! I could have searched everywhere and not found anyone who brings the spark you bring. And here you were . . . right here.

JESSIE   Waiting for you to arrive and raise me up from my ignorance! That's what my life was!

JIM   If you want to approach things in a different way tell me! There must be no barriers!

(*He wants to embrace her but her look prevents it.*)

JESSIE   There have to be some . . .

JIM   None!

JESSIE   She's my friend.

JIM   You mean ally . . . against me. I married too young, Jessie. I was keeping my family before I was twenty. I was the bread winner. They all depended on me . . . my mother and younger brothers. When I met Grace it was like sunlight is to a prisoner in a cell.

JESSIE   She's so beautiful . . .

JIM   That's what disarmed me . . .

JESSIE   What a shame you didn't meet me first . . . you
            wouldn't have had that problem!

JIM   Wouldn't I? I only have to see you create things
            to love you.

JESSIE   Not allowed. Sorry Mister. Not permitted.

JIM   I have to!

JESSIE   Love isn't in my book any more. I've torn that
            page out. I won't let myself be swallowed up like
            that. I loved a boy once. For two whole months
            the world stopped dead. There was only him and
            the pain of it. It's a kind of death.

JIM   It's life!

JESSIE   It's darkness! My pig of a father loved my silly
            mother a thousand times but gave her no life or
            light. But you bring light! I mean it. You have
            opened my eyes and I do want to work with you.
            So don't put me in darkness. Don't make me love.
            Make me see.

JIM   Then we have to be closer . . .

JESSIE   Closer? I've hardly ever been more than three
            feet from your side all these months! We sit here
            working in the afternoons and I don't know if it's
            your breathing I'm hearing or mine. Don't make
            me love!

JIM   You say it as though you could . . .

JESSIE   No!

            (*He takes her by the shoulders.*)

            Love? I'd sooner fight!

(*She slaps him.*)

You said fight. Alright! I'll fight you.

JIM   I said fight me with arguments.

JESSIE   I haven't any so I'll fight you with fight!

(*She pushes at him violently.*)

I used to do a lot of fighting! I used to fight at home. Fight with my father. Fight my brothers and sisters. Everyone says fight! Fight for justice and the new society! Fight for peace! They even say that! Fight for peace!

(*As she pommels him brushes and papers go flying off the desks.*)

Fight the good fight with all thy might!

JIM   I can't, Jessie . . .

(*He is beginning to catch his breath.* JESSIE *misunderstands. The fighting is a release for her.*)

JESSIE   Yes you can! You of all people. How is the future going to come about without a fight?

(*She thumps him in the chest. He goes down on one knee, breathing hard.*)

Are you hurt?

(*He shakes his head and concentrates on steady breathing.*)

I'm so stupid. I can't say what I mean without I lash out! Shall I get you something?

(*He shakes his head.*)

JIM   Just stay still . . .

JESSIE	What's wrong?
JIM	These lungs. Fighting or making love . . . it's all the same to them.
JESSIE	Quiet. Quiet. Don't speak.
JIM	Do they mean the same for you?
JESSIE	What happens if you smother it? Kill it? Do you end up with none left?
	(*As she kneels beside him the door opens and* HECTOR *peers in.*)
HECTOR	I heard objects falling, did I not?
JIM	Yes . . .
JESSIE	We knocked over some things . . .
	(*She tidies up.*)
JIM	Tripped myself up I'm afraid. We were just looking at Pines . . . The new design. We should be getting the new shapes fired up this week and we'll see how it goes.
HECTOR	As long as I know that no one's injured. I mustn't interrupt your dedication.
	(JESSIE *becomes irritated by his tone and inference. She puts on her things for home. On the way out she glances at the sketch.*)
JESSIE	No, I'm going. I expect you want to talk. (*To* JIM.) The pines lean away from the lightning because they're afraid of being struck by it. Goodnight Mr Brabant!
	(*She exits.*)
HECTOR	Goodnight Jessie! (*Then, to* JIM.) We mustn't be too friendly, must we?

JIM	Must we not?
HECTOR	There are quite a few temptations. Oh don't let me be mealy-mouthed - I feel it. So many young females about the place. But we must toe a certain line. Especially you and I, bound hand and foot. A certain distance - that's the art of Managing.
JIM	Yes, it must be.
HECTOR	I'm so pleased about the London prize. We've never won a prize here since my father's time. Pappa! He'd have said, "One for the cabinet".

(*A pause while* HECTOR *musters what he really wants to say.*)

	I saw a letter signed by you in the Manchester Guardian. From two days ago . . . I was shown it. I never see the Guardian. It was about the forthcoming election.
JIM	That's right.
HECTOR	You never told me it was going to appear.
JIM	I thought you didn't want politics talked about this side of the lamp post by the main gate.
HECTOR	You could have spoken in London. In any case, this is different. Arnold Savage showed it to me, so it's being talked about in the sales office. A member of the Pottery Manufacturer's Federation asked me how many more Bolsheviks had I got at Brabants.
JIM	Does he know what a Bolshevik is?
HECTOR	I'm sure you could tell him. Please be careful. I wouldn't want anything said outside about this firm . . . in the political way. And I certainly wouldn't want anything said on the premises. The point about Labour politics, Jim, is that they'll use

it to take advantage of you - every workman will
feel he has a hold over you. D'you see?

(*He smiles to take away the pressure on* JIM, *then
looks around.*)

Oh goodness! Light fades. Twilight steals. I must
wend. I must hie me home. The day is over.

(*He is about to go then picks up the Pines
sketch.*)

(*uncertainly*) Yes . . .

(*The lights fade.*)

Scene Two

A cemetery in the Potteries. JESSIE *stands by a grave. Presently*
MAB *joins her.*

MAB   Is that the one?

JESSIE   Yes.

MAB   Not much of a grave.

JESSIE   Not much of a man, was he?

             (MAB *works out the dates on the headstone.*)

MAB   He was younger than I thought.

JESSIE   He let himself be older.

MAB   Oh Lord! This cemetery goes on forever . . .

JESSIE   Like those inside it.

MAB   I've no time for burial. It takes up too much room.
             Look at the gravestones on the hill! So many
             dead . . .

JESSIE	Well there's bound to be more of them than there are of us. They get a good view of Burslem . . .
MAB	And when the wind's right they'll get the smoke.
JESSIE	So he's sleeping by the kilns like he used to. He once said that when you slept by a kiln you woke up a changed person, just as a pot comes out changed from the firing.
MAB	He never changed . . . except to go downwards.

(*She realises the double meaning and regrets it.* JESSIE *smiles.*)

JESSIE	There's one or two from our street round here. This is the end of all their work and fretting . . . the knocking up and getting out . . . lighting fires and black leading hearths.
MAB	Mangling!
JESSIE	Dolly pegging! Mopping and scrubbing and step-stoning steps! And, you see, all the effort to keep the dirt at bay and it all drifts back for the last trumpet. Even common stone's black marble here. Grey lilies and chrysanthemums the colour of ash. Smoke on Stench! You grimy towns. You smutty streets and pitch-black bricks! Is all the soot we didn't breathe when we were alive going to settle on us when we're dead?
MAB	What was it you felt for him?
JESSIE	I ask myself that. At first it was fear. I was afraid of him. I was afraid of his name. They say his mother was a foreign woman. He used to call for my father and always wait in the scullery, staring at me in the kitchen. And I'd sometimes find him standing down at the corner where we'd be playing round the street lamp. He had a stick. I learned later it was for hitting rats with in the old bakehouse where he slept. He'll like it here. Everyone sleeps rough.

MAB	Did he never have a home?
JESSIE	Oh yes . . . once. And a wife for a while.
MAB	No children surely?
JESSIE	No. He used to say she'd cheated him out of his navy pension so he left her. (*Pause.*) He'd always say something to me as I passed. Usually something I'd find upsetting. What was I going to do with my life? Didn't want me to work in pottery. Oh no! "They wusner work in a potbonk wut?" And that became a secret between us, because he knew that, if I'd told our father he'd said that, Ulik'd be bought no more beer. Yet he only said these things to me. Not my brothers. Anyway, whoever asked a girl "what are you going to do with your life?" Everybody assumed that they knew. But then I twigged. He'd seen me painting. So then I could answer him. "I want to paint pictures." And that became another secret for a while. Later it was an embarrassment. By then the praise I looked for was from clever people . . . not clodhoppers!
MAB	It's all very well for him to want others to do impossible things. He was beyond it.
JESSIE	That was his strength! People are so desperate about roofs over their head. He didn't care! Everyone'd say, where does he sleep? Where does he sleep?
MAB	He was a tramp!
JESSIE	He wasn't! Tramps move on. He lived amongst us. And all the things we go on about and worry about and clutter ourselves with . . . he just shed!
MAB	Well, you've seen his grave. You've been here. You've said what you've had to say and I've listened. Now I hope you can leave what's troubling you in here because lately you've been

hurting yourself for no good reason so far as I can see.

(JESSIE *is at first startled then almost amused at* MAB'S *concern.*)

JESSIE   Oh Mab! There's nothing wrong with me. Nothing wrong!

MAB   You're too much alone.

JESSIE   But I work. When you're away, I work. I'm alright.

MAB   Don't you see anyone?

JESSIE   Not much.

MAB   Men?

JESSIE   No.

MAB   I know I run men down sometimes but I don't cut myself off.

JESSIE   I wish I didn't have to.

MAB   Why do you?

JESSIE   To work. Brabants doesn't leave me that much time. Have you looked at what I've done lately? I've filled the place!

MAB   Then take a rest from it . . .

JESSIE   Just when I'm beginning to get the grasp of it. No!

(*They hear* GRACE *calling at a distance.*)

GRACE   (*off*) Jessie! Mab! Jessie!

(MAB *has to blow her nose.*)

MAB   Grace!

| JESSIE | I thought she said she didn't dare come in a graveyard. (*Calls.*) Over here! |

(MAB *regrets the interruption. Enter* GRACE, *very nervous.*)

| GRACE | Oh I thought you'd been swallowed up! I couldn't stay out there. I was sitting in the car and I swear I saw a ghost. An old woman in a shawl. |

| JESSIE | Where? |

| GRACE | On the pavement . . . outside the main gates. |

| JESSIE | A ghost? Outside on the pavement? |

| GRACE | Why not? They'd have to come in and out, wouldn't they? |

| JESSIE | What d'you think they do . . . clock on? |

| GRACE | I came to find you. I was alright till I saw a man with a shovel. Oh they should do away with this and have cremation. |

| MAB | I agree with you there. |

| GRACE | The flowers have withered on his grave. You should have brought some. |

| JESSIE | I couldn't bring flowers. I've brought something else though . . . |

| MAB | What? |

| JESSIE | I thought I was going to be here alone. |

(*She takes from her bag a chemist's bottle of meths.*)

I had to say I was taking up French polishing to get this!

| MAB | Is it real? |

(JESSIE *uncorks it and gives her a sniff.* MAB *recoils.*)

GRACE   You can't leave that on the grave.

JESSIE   No . . . not the bottle. Just what's in it. I'll pour it on . . .

MAB   Jessie! That's a desecration!

JESSIE   You're not religious . . .

MAB   I am here!

GRACE   Well I say 'pour it'. It's all he ever did.

(JESSIE *pours the meths over the grave.*)

JESSIE   Ulik . . . this is a gift for you in the other world. I still hear you. I do listen.

(MAB *reacts keenly to this.* JESSIE *changes her mood and speaks to* GRACE.)

Right! Put a match to that and you'll have your cremation.

(*The three of them suddenly see the funny side of it.* JESSIE *gets a match and strikes it.*)

GRACE   Oh dear! Oh dear! Don't! Don't!

(*She knocks the match from* JESSIE's *hand.*)

MAB   We'd better go before someone sees us . . .

GRACE   Come on. We'll go for a drive and blow the ghosts away.

(*As they are about to go* MAB *takes the empty bottle from* JESSIE.)

MAB   You don't want to be seen with that. Throw it away!

(*She throws it away off-stage.*)

There . . . gone!

(*They exit. The lights fade.*)

Scene Three

The freehand paint shop. JOYCE, ADA *and* VIOLET *are in full song as they work. Presently a male voice is added as* RAYMOND *backs in through the door with a tray of colours he's been told to mix. While the singing continues,* ADA *checks his mix and he hands round the paint, then takes his place at* VIOLET'S *old bench.* VIOLET *now sits in* JESSIE'S *place.*

ADA	(*shouts above the singing*) How many more, Joyce?
	(JOYCE *checks the remaining plates to be done on her bench.*)
JOYCE	Two!
ADA	Vi!
VIOLET	One!
JOYCE	(*as the song ends*) Doesn't sound the same with a man.
VIOLET	A boy!
JOYCE	He's got a terribly low voice for his age. You'll have to try to blend in more, Raymond.
RAYMOND	I was too low down. I think I'm more of a tenor, really.
JOYCE	They sing the love songs.
	(RAYMOND *smiles to himself. Enter* JESSIE, *in a hurry.*)

JESSIE	How are we Ada?
ADA	Not far off. Joyce?
JOYCE	This one . . .
ADA	Violet?
VIOLET	People keep talking.
JOYCE	Shall we be starting pines?
JESSIE	Yes we shall Joyce. The moment is at hand . . .
	(JESSIE *collects a sample in a box and checks it.*)
	I just have to take this into the meeting . . .
JOYCE	You sound cheerful. Are things going well?
JESSIE	Oh . . . not the meeting. Someone's bought two of my paintings? I'll tell you later!
	(*As she passes* RAYMOND's *bench she glances at the spray he's painting.*)
	Let me see. Yes, yes . . . lighter at the tips, otherwise that's fine.
	(*She exits.*)
ADA	You didn't show it me . . .
RAYMOND	I was going to . . .
	(*He goes to show her.*)
ADA	Oh, not now! Who cares what I think?
	(JOYCE *and* VIOLET *have been pondering* JESSIE's *bit of news.*)
VIOLET	What would she get for a painting?

JOYCE   Have you ever seen any of them, Ada?

ADA   Jessie's pictures? Not for a long time.

JOYCE   Mab asked me to look in on her. The place is full
             of them!

ADA   What are they like?

JOYCE   They worried me.

ADA   Doesn't she still paint trees?

JOYCE   Yes, but . . . Oh you'd have to see them . . .
             They're wonderfully done but she paints trees
             where the trunks are like bones . . . jointed . . .
             and knuckled. Some have veins. Not creepers . . .
             veins like you've got on your wrist.

             (*All work in silence for a while.*)

ADA   (*to* RAYMOND) Were there two more packets of
             the blue?

RAYMOND   Yes. D'you want them?

ADA   No. Just working out what we'll need . . .

JOYCE   A picture should make us feel better for looking
             at it. It should take us away from the ugliness of
             life. We know that's there. I seen enough sights
             looking after my own brother.

             (ADA *has finished her last plate.*)

ADA   I'm up.

JOYCE   Not far off.

ADA   We should sort ourselves out for pines.

JOYCE   We should cost it first. I'm talking about what we
             should get. Jessie said plates were eighteens. I'd
             say sixteens.

VIOLET	Raymond's mystified.
JOYCE	Piece rates! You don't have to worry yet till you're off the apprentice rate but you should know how we cost them. First you decide how difficult the pattern is. Then you say, I can do a dozen items in that pattern for fivepence, say. But you can do more small plates than big plates. So you might do nineteen small plates to the dozen, but only fourteen big. D'you see? You've heard of going at it nineteen to the dozen, haven't you? Well that's what you do here. (JESSIE *enters.*) Oh Jessie, duck . . . we were just discussing the money and I think we all agree there's more to do in Pines than there was in Tulips, so Pines should be sixpence, not fivepence.
JESSIE	Ada?
ADA	We were only thinking about it.
JOYCE	What is there to think about? More time in the pattern . . . more money. Otherwise we're not going to make our wages by the end of the week are we? I mean the pattern does take more time, Jessie.
JESSIE	No, I can see that.
ADA	I'm not going to be a party to asking for more . . . but I can't manage with less. We could do the pattern simpler. These two strokes green instead of blue.
JESSIE	(*lightly*) Oh no. It should stay like it is. (*She exits to the inner office and stares bleakly at the desk.*)
JOYCE	(*to* ADA) You see? Ask and it shall be given.

ACT TWO

(*They busy themselves to get working on Pines.*
RAYMOND *does the banding round the rim of the
plates - He has done some already to be started
on -* ADA, JOYCE *and* VIOLET *work round the
plates applying the Pines pattern. Presently* JIM
*enters and storms through to the inner office. He
shuts the door behind him.*)

JIM   Who does he think he is? The all-seeing and
unknowable God? He should be apologising to us
for sitting on this firm for five years and letting it
stagnate when the need for change was blaring in
his ears. And now he is telling us what shapes we
should have and what shapes we shouldn't as
though tongues of fire had descended on him on
his way to Burslem this morning. (*He struggles
with his breathing, then nods towards the painting
shop.*) I see they're on Pines.

(*He watches her, amused.*)

You spoke well at the meeting.

JESSIE   I only said one word.

JIM   Two. You said "Not really." When Savage asked
if the Pines could be a lighter shade. You said
"Not really." (*Laughs.*) "Not really!" That
sneeped him! "Not really!" He waited, thinking
you might say something else, and you didn't!

(*He opens his diary.*)

The Friday after the election . . . a week on
Friday I'm giving a speech to the Society of
Industrial Artists. I'd like you to come and I'd like
to put you up for membership. You're not going
to say "Not really"?

JESSIE   I don't know much about it.

JIM   I was writing the speech last night. I thought,
because of the reputation I'm getting as a red, I'd
open by saying   "Colleagues . . . ". Then I'll

look around the room as though noting one or two of the members there and add "Comrades . . . ?

(*He gets no response from her.* JESSIE'S *mind is on other things.*)

Make a joke of it. (*Pause.*) Did you talk about the piece work rate for Pines?

JESSIE   Joyce and Ada think it should be more than Tulips.

JIM   But I told you to get in first . . .

JESSIE   Pines takes longer than Tulips.

JIM   But Tulips was overpriced! You know what the point is. We've done good designs but the ware is only selling through the middle class shops. That's not where we want to see the product of our minds, Jessie. I want to see our ideas taken up by working class people and to do that the price has to be kept down. Look . . . I'll have a go, I need to try and catch Brabant now he's back in his office, see if I can get some sense out of him. While I'm gone, I suggest you have a word. I'm looking to you to manage this shop before long so I can turn my attention to the litho and transfer.

(*He exits to the shop and stops to examine* JOYCE'S *work.*)

Ah! Pines . . . that colour's working well! First prize again!

JOYCE   (*assuming he's agreed the prices*) Nothing'll stop us!

JIM   Oh . . . and everyone let me remind you . . . General Election next week. Our chance to change the government. Well, now you've got the vote, I trust you're not going to use it like sheep.

JOYCE   Why? What do sheep vote for?

RAYMOND   Grass.

JOYCE   Heyup!

JIM   Well if they're really intelligent they would vote
               for grass. So should we all. And yet, Raymond,
               you'd be surprised how many vote for the
               abattoir . . . but I am not supposed to discuss
               politics on the premises . . . (*He leans close to*
               JOYCE.) . . . so if you want my opinions, we will
               have to meet after hours just past the first lamp
               post outside the main gate. (*He beams at*
               everyone and exits.)

ADA   What was that all about?

JOYCE   I think it was an offer. Oh, when he puts his face
               close to mine - and all the rest of him attached to
               it! I may not be open to persuasion where my
               vote's concerned but I could be open to bribery.

VIOLET   He's been told by Mr Brabant.

ADA   What has he been told? (*She knows but wants to*
               know how far it has got.)

VIOLET   Not to talk political.

ADA   Who says?

JOYCE   Oh Ada! Everyone! It's common knowledge.

ADA   Well I wish it weren't. To me politics is a private
               and personal matter. How I cast my vote will
               remain a total secret.

JOYCE   You mean even you won't know?

ADA   Can we get on with the work, please?

JOYCE   I think he's agreed.

ADA   How d'you know?

JOYCE   Well . . . he was cheerful enough.

(*They all concentrate on their work for a while. In the inner office,* JESSIE *writes a note of resignation. She thinks of putting it on* JIM'S *desk, then puts it in her bag. Slowly and mingled with the concentration on the work,* JOYCE *leads a chorus that grows a little more cheerful as it progresses.* JESSIE *listens, feeling the distance growing between her and them.*)

JOYCE   (*sings*) "We are the freehand painters
Happy boys and girls . . . "

(*Others join in gradually to the "Ovaltiny" tune.*)

"All day long we're decorating
And for work we're always waiting
Bands, lines, leaves and petals
Zig-zags, dots and curls
For hours and hours
We're painting flowers
We're happy boys and girls!"

ADA   We'll want more green Raymond . . .

JOYCE   Now . . . before he does that . . . this is the first pattern you've been in on from the start isn't it?

RAYMOND   Yes . . .

JOYCE   Well, you'll have to be whatsited . . .

ADA   Oh, don't waste time!

JOYCE   There are some things that are more important, Ada. Tradition and custom must be observed. Everyone has to go through it . . . what's it called?

VIOLET   Initiation.

JOYCE   Initiation. Your ceremony. You'd better have it done by us than the men. You don't want to be at the mercy of the saggar maker's bottom knockers.

VIOLET   The women in the pressing shop are worst. Did
                you hear what they did to one of the boys?

ADA   No and we don't want to!

VIOLET   You know those big baskets in there. They get a
                boy standing with his back to it . . . give him a
                push and once he's in there lying on his back . . .
                he's helpless.

JOYCE   We'll strike a bargain since I happen to be in the
                mood. You will be counted as fully initiated if you
                give each of us a kiss. And I mean on the lips.

VIOLET   Is that all? That's not fair.

JOYCE   It'll do me. What about it Ada?

ADA   He doesn't want to do that . . .

JOYCE   Of course he does . . . and for that remark you
                can be first . . . and don't hold back or he'll feel
                unwanted.

                (RAYMOND *is not too abashed. He turns to* ADA.)

ADA   Well do it if you're going to!

JOYCE   Be careful of Ada. Her fiancee's a dental
                technician and kisses like a suction pump.

ADA   Joyce . . .

                (*But* RAYMOND *makes an awkward lunge and
                suddenly kisses her on the mouth. At this moment*
                JESSIE *enters the shop from the inner office.*)

JOYCE   We're initiating him Jessie. Don't look down your
                nose, it's your turn presently. Violet.

                (VIOLET *grabs* RAYMOND *by the ears and kisses
                him viciously.* RAYMOND *pulls back, hurt, and
                rubs his mouth.*)

You've not drawn blood have you?

VIOLET   Let's see . . .

(*She goes to inspect* RAYMOND'S *mouth then quickly dabs paint on his lip.*)

JOYCE   You vixen! Wipe it off. And wipe your lips where she's been. We'll show them how it should be done.

(*She folds his arms around her and kisses as in the movies.*)

JOYCE   Oooo! You can certainly hold your breath!

RAYMOND   I swim under water.

JOYCE   How far can you do?

RAYMOND   A length.

JOYCE   Any length?

VIOLET   (*indicates* JESSIE) Her now Raymond! Her turn!

JESSIE   Don't look so worried. You don't have to.

(*But* RAYMOND *is drawn to* JESSIE. *He walks over to her and they kiss gently and tenderly. As they draw back* JESSIE *stares at him in anguish. She begins to shudder violently.*)

JOYCE   What's up?

ADA   What's he done?

(*They go to steady her.*)

JESSIE   I shan't fall. I shan't go over. Standing on my own feet's what I'm good at! Me fall? Never! I'm sorry Raymond . . . it wasn't you.

> (*She is given some water to drink and led slowly into the inner office to her desk.* JOYCE *is alone with her.*)

JOYCE   It's all too much for you duck . . .

JESSIE   I wish I was that boy. To be back at the start with your life an open book!

JOYCE   Sit quiet. Have a moment.

> (*She rejoins the others in the paint shop.*)

               I've seen that coming.

ADA   I thought she was going to faint.

RAYMOND   (*trying to calm himself*) I fainted once. They brought a doctor to me. I woke with him looking down at me. But he said I was alright. He says everyone's allowed a faint or two so long as they don't come close together . . .

ADA   Can we please concentrate on what we're supposed to be doing?

> (*They all go back to their work in a subdued way. The lights feature* JESSIE *as she stares ahead of her then suddenly senses a presence.*)

JESSIE   Ulik?

> (*Unseen by those in the outer office the ghost of* ULIK *walks through and stands alongside* JESSIE.)

               I'm not going to have the will to do it . . .

ULIK   Yes they at.

JESSIE   I'll fail.

ULIK   No, they wusner.

JESSIE   I will! I'll fall down on it!

ULIK   They wusner.

JESSIE   It all seems so cold ahead. I feel my summer's
              been and gone.

ULIK   They't ardly left off being a wench . . . a little girl
              painting her first strokes. Well, if summer's gone,
              fly! It's no use here. Never can be . . . for here
              they kostner be thi'sen. Be thi'sen. Be no other
              but thi'sen. It's hard I know. The hardest thing in
              the creation is to make thi'self be what they't
              created for. But what must be fulfilled must be
              fulfilled. Be thi'sen.

JESSIE   Then help me!

ULIK   Help thee? What else are the dead for? The
              dead'll help thee. The dead help them as dare to
              live . . . for most who die, die stripped of pride
              and wishing they'd lived life more strongly . . .
              and when they see one like Jessie Frost who
              dares to be hersen, it warms them like a red hot
              coal in the earth. Dare to do it and they't have a
              graveyard full of helpers. They't have cemeteries
              of friends!

JESSIE   I have the note.

ULIK   In thy bag . . . I know. Put it for him. Put it theer.
              Put it where he'll see it, when he comes.

              (JESSIE *makes a great effort and gets the sealed
              envelope from her bag and props it on* JIM'S
              desk.)

              Now . . . live as they wust. Be thi'sen and be no
              other.

              (*He begins to go.*)

JESSIE   Ulik? (*He pauses.*) What's death like?

ULIK   I can no more say what death's like than they kost
              tell me what life's like. And life has an end. Death

doesn't. But Death is kind. In all that darkness, he saves me a little bit of blue.

(*He goes back the way he came. Lights return to normal. The mid-day hooters sound.*)

JOYCE   There! How bright it is suddenly! Come on who's coming and let's eat our snappin in the yard . . . (*Pops her head round* JESSIE'S *door.*) Jessie?

JESSIE   I'll follow you down . . .

(JOYCE *rejoins the others.*)

Leave her. (*To* RAYMOND.) She'll follow.

(*She picks up her lunch and notices* VIOLET *hanging back at her bench.*)

Violet . . .

VIOLET   In a bit.

(JOYCE *gives her a suspicious look then all exit, except* VIOLET. *While* JESSIE *sits silent in the inner office,* VIOLET *undoes her folder of designs that she nurses to herself. She begins to work on one, in deep concentration.* JESSIE *picks up the letter and almost seems at one point as though she would take it back and hide it away. Then she makes a decision, picks up her lunch and is about to go. At this moment* JIM *blazes into the outer shop and stalks right through, not giving* VIOLET *a glance.*)

JIM   (*to* JESSIE) None! Not one! No new shapes till we've covered the increased costs of this department. No investment! No foresight! No guts! And then we had an almighty ding-dong about him refusing to let the union hold a works meeting. He said it'd turn into an election meeting. I said "why not?" I tell you what Jessie - I'll call one myself. I'll get 'em all out in the yard there and we'll take hold of the freedom to speak that we're

supposed to have under our benighted and
mysterious constitution. And he's free to bring his
Tory friends and heckle us. Heckling Hector! Eh?
"Friends . . . colleagues . . . comrades!"

(*His eye falls on the letter on his desk. He
guesses the contents but takes out the note of
resignation slowly and reads it in silence.* JESSIE
lets him finish, then speaks softly.)

JESSIE   I have an aunt in Derbyshire, in Matlock Spa.
She's widowed and she keeps a shop. Souvenirs
for tourists. I don't know if you know Matlock . . .

(*He makes no gesture.*)

She likes my paintings and when she was last in
Stoke she took two of them to try and sell . . . in
her shop. Months went by. I'd given up. Then
she writes. Encloses a postal order. She's sold
them both to the same person . . . a woman who
wanted them for her sister's birthday. I'd never
thought of what I did as being a birthday present!
And my aunt said what she'd said before . . . that I
could up sticks and move there . . . live there . . .
look after the shop four mornings a week for my
keep . . . and the rest of my time I'd have for
painting! There's quite a barn of a room where I
can sleep and work.

(*A pause.* JIM *doesn't move.*)

I don't know how you'll want it done. When you'll
want me to go.

JIM   I've felt this blow coming so often I've lost the will
to ward it off.

JESSIE   You're going to be so blazing with me . . .

JIM   If you go it's no use . . .

JESSIE   I won't weaken. I won't.

JIM	Just when the tide is flowing in our favour.
JESSIE	That's not what you were saying just now . . .
JIM	I mean in England!
JESSIE	This isn't about politics.
JIM	Everything's about politics!
JESSIE	Not this . . .
JIM	We should have discussed the issues more . . .
JESSIE	This isn't about politics. It's about me! What I must do. Politics is always about them . . . what they must do!
JIM	(*shakes his head*) What we must do . . .
JESSIE	We? Not so much of that this morning when we talked about piece rates. Making our designs cheap enough for working class people by getting working women to take less for the painting. That was them!
JIM	There have to be sacrifices along the way. Change doesn't come gently. It's no soft option.
JESSIE	Oh tell that to the works! Tell the men through there. (*Points.*) And the women in there! Tell them about the sacrifices they'll have to make for change! You can argue. I can't. You tell em how we're going to change the world with our tea sets!
JIM	D'you think it makes me happy that we have to drag ourselves through the market place to get where we want to be? You have a point about the rates. I know you have. We'll talk. We'll discuss it.
JESSIE	I want to paint . . .
JIM	Then paint here! We could have an arrangement. Design and paint! Anything's possible. All I ask is

that we still share our work. I know you share the
same principles . . . even though you won't say
so. You can't be a traitor to that part of yourself.
You can't let yourself be guided by some
wayward compass swinging blindly about in the
mind!

(JESSIE *is infuriated by the implication that her
choice is arbitrary.*)

JESSIE   I won't!

(*She exits. For a moment or two* JIM *is beaten.
But then a thought strikes him. He becomes his
old positive self again. He grabs a note pad and
starts scribbling points for a speech. He opens his
case and refers to a newspaper cutting from it. He
grins, lifts* JESSIE's *letter . . . then jots down a
quote.*)

JIM   "Change the world with our tea sets."

(*During this,* VIOLET *makes up her mind to take
advantage of there being no one else around.
She gathers her designs into her folder and
crosses to the inner office door.*)

VIOLET   Mr Rhys . . .

JIM   (*reluctantly*) What's that?

VIOLET   I've done some patterns. Would you look at
                them?

(*But at this moment* RAYMOND *appears,
breathless.*)

RAYMOND   Jessie forgot her bag . . .

JIM   Oh did she?

RAYMOND   Can I get it?

JIM   You can . . . and more than that you can do
                       something for me . . . you're the very man! On
                       your way back to Jessie I want you to do a
                       lightning tour of the works as fast as you know
                       how. You run as well as swim don't you?

RAYMOND   Yes, sir . . .

JIM   Get round to everyone . . . our fettlers and
                       finishers, jolliers and jiggerers, saggar and slip
                       makers, glazers and glost house workers and all
                       the other inspired lunatics we employ in this
                       cough and spit industry . . . tell them to come to
                       the unloading yard now where Jim Rhys will be
                       giving a speech concerning the forthcoming
                       election and who we should all vote for. Don't
                       forget the sales office . . . and Raymond . . .

RAYMOND   Yes, Mr Rhys . . .

JIM   The Traveller's Rest over the road . . . get 'em
                       out!

RAYMOND   Yes sir!

JIM   Go to it!

                       (RAYMOND, *elated, hares away. We hear his
                       excited voice down the corridor.*)

RAYMOND   (*off*) Mr Tunnicliffe!

TUNNICLIFFE   (*off*) Heyup!

RAYMOND   (*off*) Mr Rhys is doing a Labour election speech
                       in the unloading yard in three minutes!

TUNNICLIFFE   (*off*) Hey inner izzy?

WOMAN   (*more distant*) What at on about?

                       (*We hear* RAYMOND *repeat a similar message
                       faintly and several women whoop with glee.* JIM
                       chuckles to himself. He grabs his notes. As he

glances through and makes additions, VIOLET
*quickly lays out her designs on the nearest
bench, desperate for him to look at them.* JIM *tries
his speech.*)

JIM   Colleagues! (*He pretends to look for fellow
travellers in the crowd.*) Comrades! Friends!
Foes? Fellow Brabant-ites! Next week we go to
the polls . . .

(*He makes another note and looks as though he's
about to go.*)

VIOLET   Mr Rhys! When will you have time to look?

JIM   Oh, sooner than you think, Violet. But it may have
to be beyond the first lamp post past the main
gates.

(*He exits.* VIOLET *is angry and stricken. From
outside in the yard we hear cheers and laughter.
A cracked bugle is blown. Through it all comes
the old election song to the tune of "Tramp,
tramp, tramp, the boys are marching" with the
words: "Vote, vote, vote, for Jimmy Rhys, lads!
He's the one that we adore! And if we get him in,
We'll hit him on the chin . . . And he won't go a-
voting any more!" Tearfully,* VIOLET *shuffles her
designs together.* HECTOR BRABANT *enters.*)

HECTOR   Have you seen Mr Rhys?

(*A cheer from below.*)

VIOLET   He's in the yard sir. Making a speech.

(BRABANT *stands stiffly listening as* JIM *gets under
way.*)

JIM   (*off*) Can you hear me properly?

(*A big "Yes" and the odd "No" from the crowd.*)

Colleagues! (*Laughter.*) Comrades? (*A big laugh. As* JIM *continues with his speech, only just audible,* VIOLET *sizes up* HECTOR *and in her desperation lays out her drawings once more.*)

VIOLET   Sir . . . sir. I've done some patterns. Would you have a look?

(*But* BRABANT'S *eyes see nothing as he stares ahead and listens in anger and despair.*)

JIM   (*off*) Next week we go to the polls . . . to prove that Stoke-on-Trent is not where the mugs come from . . . (*Laughter.*) We may not be able to change the world with our tea sets . . . but we can make sure that there's a fair and proper share out of the cake! . . .

(*The lights fade.*)

Scene Four

The garden of the Pines, about one month later . . . September.

GRACE, *in a smart, fashionable suit is tying a scrap of knotted rope round some old garden tools to hold them together on the move. Some tea chests stand at the back of the house. The dog barks.* RAYMOND *enters wearing cycle clips.*

GRACE   Are you Raymond?

RAYMOND   Yes . . . I came to say they won't be long.

(*More barking off stage.*)

GRACE   Take no notice of Marx. He's a bit lost today. (*To the dog.*) You needn't give me that expression. Yes . . . you're going on a journey you know not where!

(GRACE *sizes him up.*)

So you're the one that kisses the girls . . .

(RAYMOND *smiles.*)

RAYMOND   That's me.

GRACE   Don't you get fed up with that roomful of women?

RAYMOND   I like women.

GRACE   Oh do you! What d'you like about them?

RAYMOND   I like the colours they wear.

(GRACE *is surprised by the reply. She indicates her blouse.*)

GRACE   D'you like this?

RAYMOND   (*nods*) I do. Yes.

GRACE   It's French. Shantung. I shouldn't be wearing it but if my whole life's going to be bundled up in brown paper parcels again I need something . . .

RAYMOND   Are those the pines?

GRACE   Yes. There looks a lot of them but there aren't, really. He used to talk as though they went all the way from here to Russia. But there's only a thin narrow strip of them to where the old wood begins, that's all. Just a piece of scenery. And they'll all be chopped down when they're a little bit bigger. Just something you could paint on a cloth and then say: "I don't like that. Scrub it off!"

RAYMOND   I broke a window.

GRACE   Where?

RAYMOND   At Brabants. When I heard what had happened to Mr Rhys. I thought I'd go round breaking windows . . .

GRACE   How many did you break?

RAYMOND   Only the one.

GRACE   D'you get in trouble?

RAYMOND   No. There's always a lot broken. They never
               noticed. I think his speech was the most cleverest
               thing I've ever heard.

GRACE   It must have been. He's talked us into nowhere
               with it.

               (*They hear a car arriving.* GRACE *suddenly feels
               a sense of apprehension.*)

               Is Jessie with them?

RAYMOND   Yes. Mab drove them to get her from the station.

               (JOYCE *enters almost on tiptoe.*)

JOYCE   Where is he?

GRACE   Inside . . .

               (JOYCE *beckons and* ADA *enters with a big
               presentation dish wrapped in special paper.* MAB
               follows with JESSIE, *white and tense.*)

JOYCE   It's our present . . .

ADA   Don't tell her!

JOYCE   For both of you . . .

               (GRACE *hugs them.*)

GRACE   (*to* MAB) Nothing lasts! You in Leeds . . . us in
               Birmingham, it looks like.

MAB   It's settled is it?

GRACE   (*nods and turns to embrace* JESSIE) And you in
               Derbyshire . . . we might as well be in foreign
               lands!

MAB   Nonsense. We can drive to see each other.

JESSIE   Me? You can. I'll be lucky to afford a new pair of
                    shoes.

MAB   Persuade her, Grace. Stop her going! Tell her it's
                    a trap. I know what that aunt of hers wants . . .
                    I've seen this so often . . . nieces and daughters.
                    Stay unmarried and they're on to you. They'll
                    have you to skivvy and scrub and slave away!
                    Her aunt just wants a cheap body to do the work,
                    to keep house, mind the shop and see to her in
                    her old age.

JESSIE   She's not old . . .

MAB   She will be!

JOYCE   We all will be . . .

MAB   I've seen her room! I've seen the place! Dark
                    and dismal and damp. You could feel the curtains
                    sopping wet! It's not for her. She wasn't made for
                    that. She could have stayed with me . . . shared
                    with me. I'd have covered the rent till she got
                    money in. Talk her out of it . . .

                    (*There is open embarrassment at* MAB's
                    outpouring.)

GRACE   You can't tell a grown woman what to do.

                    (JIM *enters with some books.*)

JIM   Hello!

                    (JESSIE *immediately moves away and remains
                    detached from the group.* JIM *notes her presence
                    and then ignores her totally. The others become
                    conscious of the tension.*)

GRACE   Everyone's waiting!

JOYCE   Morning Mr Rhys!

JIM   Morning! Forgive me . . . I got overtaken by the
             natural law of packing books. For every six you
             pack there's one you can't stop reading. I
             managed to resist Lawrence and Wells and
             Engels . . . but I just had to take a peek at Jack
             London's short stories. "To Light A Fire" . . .
             wonderful tale about a man lost in the frozen
             wastes without a match.

GRACE   If you're cold we'll go indoors . . .

JOYCE   We're all here . . . except Violet. Oh the crawler!
             She said we should all have the sack, talking to
             you.

JIM   Is it that bad? You shouldn't have put yourselves
             in danger. Ada I'm surprised at you . . .

ADA   So am I!

             (*He shakes hands with* RAYMOND.)

JIM   Shall you ever forget that famous run?

RAYMOND   Never!

JIM   I shouldn't have involved you . . .

RAYMOND   They can do as they like!

JIM   I'm afraid that's all too true . . . And Miss Mabel
             Cooper of the other persuasion! Well you lot are
             in again. We lost. But only the battle. Not the war.

MAB   I'm more concerned with what Brabant's lost.

JIM   Bless you!

JOYCE   And Jessie's here . . .

             (JOYCE *is trying to get him to greet* JESSIE, *but* JIM
             won't acknowledge her.)

JIM   Well, I hope something survives from what we did together. Some spirit. Some thrust! We went a good way in a short time. For a while I actually think in our own fashion we blazed something of a trail . . .

(*He stops, fighting his emotion.*)

JOYCE   We have a present to give you and Mrs Rhys. Ada'll give it 'cos she's the missus.

ADA   Am I? I have no illusions on that score. I've always just got on with my work and done my best to see to matters and where management is concerned I've taken it as it comes. Tried not to let it bother me. But I never thought such a terrible thing could happen. You don't do you? You should see the freehand shop now. It's very strange. We've left the knot quite loose.

(JIM *undoes the paper and reveals a big meat dish in Pines pattern signed with a host of signatures. He shows it to* GRACE.)

JOYCE   We got everyone at the works to paint their signature . . . everyone who's worth knowing signed.

JIM   Oh this is a most momentous meat dish. This dish will be sat on our table with the deepest sense of pride. This'll see us through all the Sundays of our lives, believe me!

GRACE   We're not going to use it! We can't carve the joint on it.

JIM   Yes we can! And when the blood runs we'll think of Hector Brabant! The pines stand for Russia . . . the lightning for socialism. He calls me a red. I'm no red . . . but I'll defend one thing the Russians have done though we may not like the way they've done it. They've created the model for us to follow. Crude, yes! Needing more refinement . . . more humanity. But they're learning. They're

showing the way . . . and by the end of the
century the socialist ideal will have triumphed
right across Europe!

(*An embarrassed silence.*)

MAB   (*cutting through it*) So you are going to
Birmingham?

GRACE   The day after tomorrow.

ADA   It's so sad you leaving the Potteries.

GRACE   Oh no we're not doing that! It's the other way
round . . .

JIM   She means the Potteries are leaving us. You
obviously don't know so I'll tell you. I'm going to
work for Railtons Tiles. As consultant designer.
The reason I'm having to go outside the Potteries
is that after I got my marching orders from
Hector, he and the other employers discussed the
matter - in the Employers Federation - and I was
sent word that I needn't expect to work in Stoke-
on-Trent again.

GRACE   They blacklisted him.

JOYCE   Blacked? You're blacked?

JIM   Isn't the rumour going around?

JOYCE   If I'd heard it I wouldn't have believed it!

MAB   They can't!

JIM   They have.

MAB   They gang together like that!

JIM   There's no union like a bosses union. I'm
flattered in a way. Oh I respect them for it. My
God! If the citadels of capital didn't have to be so

savagely defended they wouldn't be worth
bringing down, would they?

MAB   Then I shall leave, too.

JOYCE   So shall I, if that's what Hector thinks he can get
away with!

(JESSIE *suddenly speaks without moving from her
isolated position.*)

JESSIE   But Brabant didn't do it. Not on his own he didn't.
(*Indicates* JIM.) He knows who's to blame! He
knows . . . oh so very well . . . who's fault it was!

(*The others are caught between the two of
them . . . her, quick, desperate, aggressive . . .
and him, never looking at her, maintaining a
steady flow of argument, but burning in his mind.*)

Bosses are bosses and will behave like bosses but
what of your own side? Your own troops? What
of some stupid, obstinate woman who wouldn't
stay on the rails just when everything was going
so well?

(JIM *never looks at her as he speaks.*)

JIM   What I did had nothing to do with anyone else . . .

JESSIE   He thinks I'm so guilty! That's why I don't exist
any more! That's why I'm not here!

JIM   There was no personal element involved . . .
except for Hector Brabant!

MAB   Where has all this sprung from?

JOYCE   I knew it! I knew she shouldn't have come.

JESSIE   He wants me to stew in it!

JIM   We were being prevented from holding an open
discussion in our own time, in our own way . . .

JESSIE   He'll go through life thinking I've been disloyal . . .

JIM   . . . Just because he didn't like the subject in
           hand. This is not a personal matter, it's a matter of
           principle.

JESSIE   And I'm wrong and he's right! And I'm wrong and
           I'm wrong and I'm wrong! When I heard he was
           sacked I thought: good! That slams the bolt on it!
           We can't backtrack now! I won't have to face
           giving way or be prey to my own soft-
           mindedness!

ADA   I can't stand this! I can't stand it when people row!
           Don't spoil the day . . .

JESSIE   Does he think I did it because I wanted to? That I
           had any choice?

JIM   We're all free to choose but the only true
           freedom is to see clearly that we are all bound
           one with another in the same community with the
           same purpose! It's in each other that we're free!

MAB   One of you has to stop! Jessie!

JESSIE   Who *can* be free? I can't! I have to tear myself up
           by the roots and paint my days away and grab and
           grasp at every inch of canvas till it's used up and
           covered!

JIM   None of us is exempt . . .

JESSIE   And turn my back . . .

JIM   None of us . . .

JESSIE   And turn my back . . .

JIM   None!

JESSIE   And turn my back on the people and the prizes
           and the good money. To lose my life with Mab.
           Our flat . . . and have to change it for ingrained

dirt and grime and rotten boards and a piss-
soaked privy by the back door! Does he think I
go to that for some non-understanding in my
head? I know what I do! Give up all he gained
for me. The chance to shine and the chance to be
right! Oh, wonderful just to put down paint on a
plate and be on the side of the angels! But I'm not
worth a moment's thought! I'm like those who
won't join the human race. Who won't be ruled or
kow-tow or bend the knee or knuckle under!
Who sleep by the kiln wall and have no roof and
drink themselves into the grave . . . and get found
in a ditch by a children's dog . . . and should be
here . . . over there . . . just there!

(*She points to the spot where* ULIK *once stood by
the woods.*)

But if he doesn't come it's past mattering now. It's
been said.

GRACE   I think it's time we went in from the garden. Come
               on indoors.

MAB   We'll take you to your train. You've done more
               than enough here.

ADA   Mrs Rhys . . . I'm sorry this has happened.

               (*But* JIM *hasn't finished.*)

JIM   There are those who say "I'm different."

GRACE   (*trying to prevent him*) Jim!

MAB   Stop!

JESSIE   Who? Who says?

JOYCE   Why go on?

ADA   Why argue?

JIM   I'm not as others are. My purpose is art . . . and
               nothing but art.

JESSIE   Art? Art? Art-fart! Art's a word! Spell it backwards
            and it says "Tra". Tra! Tra duck! Tra! Tra to art!

MAB   (*to* JESSIE) Are you determined to tear yourself in
            two, or what? Are the rest of us not worth your
            while any more? (*To* JIM.) You should have let
            her stay with her own ideas, not forced yours on
            her!

JIM   No one's exempt. We're all in the struggle.

JESSIE   Oh I'm in the struggle!

JIM   I? I? There's no "I" in it. Not "I" . . . but "us".
            That's where the struggle is.

JESSIE   I see more struggle in a flower in a field than in a
            thousand socialisms!

JIM   These mystical mumbo-jumbo mongers who think
            with their blood instead of their brains. It's time
            for them to stop avoiding the one clear question -
            How much am I for others, how much am I for
            myself?

JESSIE   I don't have to answer . . .

JIM   There was a man - two weeks ago - who said to
            me straight, "For myself". I don't grieve over him
            - not as I do over those who have so much to
            give and won't give it . . . and out of, I don't know
            what - some deep treachery to themselves - they
            think they can put themselves above the question.

            (JESSIE *shuts him out*.)

ADA   Well I have to go on working for Brabants if no
            one else does. I took a risk coming here!

JIM   She won't answer!

JESSIE   I don't have to answer!

ADA
We should go now. Thank you very much, Mrs Rhys.

RAYMOND
He's there! He's speaking the truth. Why won't she answer?

JOYCE
Raymond! Come away . . .

RAYMOND
He pretends she's not there. She's with you . . . there!

JOYCE
Leave them!

RAYMOND
But they took me in. They saw my work. They stood with me and looked at what I'd done . . . why won't they face each other now?

JOYCE
I've seen enough pain in my own life. I won't stay and see others make it up out of nothing.

MAB
Come on everyone. Jessie, we're going!

(JOYCE, MAB, ADA *and* RAYMOND *exit.* JESSIE *crosses to* GRACE. GRACE *doesn't move.*)

JESSIE
If he hadn't blown in through the door that day and wakened everything up I'd have dozed forever. When you work alongside him, you were on the high road of life! But once he set me on it I could see my way . . . I want your letters, Grace. Write to this poor fool!

(*She glances towards* JIM *but he still refuses to look at her. She exits.*)

JIM
There's only one question and they won't listen! What's happening to the world? Is it going deaf?

(*We hear the car door shut, the engine start and the car drive away.* JIM *senses, and wishes, that she might still be there.*)

Has she gone? Did she get in the car?

(GRACE *can't answer, simply seeing how much* JESSIE *meant to him.*)

We'll go. I don't want another night here. I can telephone. See if they can do it today. You never liked it. you want life and people. All this . . . silence . . . it deadens everything. Sometimes I think the only life here is the sound my lungs make. We'll live among people now. Work patiently. Make the arguments more telling. Get them across . . . they have to be persuaded . . .

(*He inspects the presentation meat dish.*)

It's wrong, this design . . . quite wrong. I said it was. The pines should lean towards the lightning . . .

(*Slow fade to black.*)